MOHAMMED

THE MAN AND HIS FAITH

TOR ANDRAE

Translated by
THEOPHIL MENZEL

HARPER TORCHBOOKS
Harper & Row, Publishers
New York, Hagerstown, San Francisco, London

MOHAMMED: The Man and His Faith

Printed in the United States of America

First published by Charles Scribner's Sons in 1936 and reprinted by arrangement with Barnes & Noble, Inc., who published this revised edition in 1955.

First HARPER TORCHBOOK edition published 1960

Library of Congress catalog card number: 60–5489

TRANSLATOR'S PREFACE

THIS volume is a translation from the German of Professor Tor Andrae's *Mohammed, Sein Leben und Sein Glaube*, published by Vandenhoeck and Ruprecht, Goettingen, 1932.

Spanish and Italian translations have also appeared.

The study of Mohammed's life and work is advancing so rapidly that no apology is needed for publishing this excellent study. We have reached the stage where it is possible to approach his personality with a measure of understanding and balance impossible of attainment a few decades ago. It is hoped that this work will appeal to students of the history of religion, lovers of biography, and adherents of Islam.

As a teacher of the history of religion I have been impressed by Professor Andrae's rare ability to present the essential fruits of recent research in a manner which is both simple and vital. In keeping with his avoidance of technicalities I have employed a system of spelling Islamic terms which may seem woefully unscholarly, but which conforms, as much as possible, to common usage.

In July 1933 *The Moslem World* printed a translation of Chapter IV of this volume, prepared by Professor Arthur Jeffery of the Columbia University at Cairo. I am greatly indebted to *The Moslem World* for permission to use this translation. The spelling has been changed to bring it into conformity with the remainder of the book.

The passages of the Koran which have been cited are taken from Rodwell's translation.

I wish to express my appreciation for the assistance and encouragement given by Professor Samuel Zwemer of Princeton, Professor Arthur Jeffery, Professor Daniel S. Robinson of Indiana University, Professor Reinhold Niebuhr of Union Theological Seminary, New York, and to the publishers.

THEOPHIL MENZEL

EDEN THEOLOGICAL SEMINARY
WEBSTER GROVES MO.
October 1935

CONTENTS

INTRODUCTION

THERE was a time when it was considered in accordance with good scientific method to interpret all religious development as due to personal forces: either to social and economic factors, which operated with the simple inevitability of natural law, or to ideas and conceptions which, by their necessary and reciprocal interaction, gave rise to religious dogmas and systems. The bearers of this development are not individual, creative personalities, but an anonymous mass: the nation, the sect, the congregation, the mystical brotherhood. No place was really left for the great, leading, creative religious personalities. To go back to the particular personal experience, or the prophetic initiative, as the source of the new religious creation, was regarded as an act of scientific bankruptcy. In many cases this tendency went to the extreme of simply denying that the great founders of religion ever lived. To be sure, genuine scholars were less liable to draw such conclusions than scientific amateurs. Nevertheless, various scientists and self-appointed critics have denied the historicity not only of Buddha and Zarathustra, but also of Jesus and Paul. The spirit of collectivism, which had won so many victories in the political and social sphere, invaded also the quiet world of the humanistic sciences.

It is certainly not a sign of a higher methodological insight to imagine history as a drama without actors, a drama in which every action is performed by dummies. In all religious movements whose history we can really survey the awakening power proceeded from an individual personality. We find the same phenomenon even in the most recent formation of sects. The master or the prophet, and his disciples: this is the ordinary cell out of which new life grows in the sphere of religion. By no means, however, need science balk at the individual personality as if it were a supernatural entity before which our research must lay down its tools. The endeavour to trace how there is created in the inner life of the genius or the prophet a new spiritual synthesis of elements, which, even though they are all 'given' in the environment, are nevertheless there isolated, without the possibility of interaction, presents a variety of fascinating problems to science before it pauses to consider the actually new factor, the secret of the creative spiritual life.

That Mohammed really lived cannot be disputed. The development of Islam—at least, as compared with the other world religions—is open to the clear light of history, and it presents us with yet another proof that the prophetic personality is the original source of the new religious creation. To be sure, it has often been said that Mohammed was definitely lacking in originality; that one cannot speak of a new creation in the case of one who appropriated so much from Judaism and Christianity. In a certain sense this is true. That the fundamental ideas of Islam were borrowed from the Biblical religions is a fact which requires no further discussion. As we shall see later, the religion of the Prophet, both in its form of expression and in its spirit, is related, even more closely than has hitherto been assumed, to the dominant piety of the Syrian churches. And yet it is cheap wisdom to think that this disposes of the question of Mohammed's originality. A new form of religious life like that of Islam is not merely a body of doctrine or a system of ritual. It is, when profoundly regarded, a form of spiritual energy, a living seed. It develops its own life and attracts other spiritual life to itself, according to a law whose significance and purpose is completely revealed only after an extended development. There is originality enough in Mohammed's achievement in catching up into a vital and adaptable personal synthesis the spiritual potentialities of his age. Truly 'My prayers and my worship and my life and my death are unto God, Lord of the Worlds. He hath no associate. This am I commanded, and I am the first of the Muslims' (Sura 6, 163). *The first of the Muslims*! Mohammed is absolutely justified in so designating himself

He is the first representative of a new and independent religious type. Even to-day, after a period of development of thirteen centuries, one may clearly discern in genuine Islamic piety the uniqueness which is ultimately derived from its founder's personal experience of God.

Hitherto the nature of Mohammedan piety has generally been rather unjustly ignored by Western students of religion. If one were to seek out the cause for this, it would not suffice to refer to ignorance, or to the reaction of old dogmatic prejudices against the 'false prophet,' or to political hatred of 'the dog of a Turk.' The cause lies deeper, and may perhaps be best expressed by the proverb: Relatives understand each other least of all. A Christian sees much in Islam which reminds him of his own religion, but he sees it in an extremely distorted form. He finds ideas and statements of belief clearly related to those of his own religion, but which, nevertheless, turn off into strangely different paths. Islam is so familiar to us that we pass it by with the careless indifference with which we ignore that which we know and know only too well. And yet it is not familiar enough to us to enable us really to understand its uniqueness, and the spirit by which Islam has won its own place in the sphere of religion, a place which it still rightly occupies by virtue of its very existence. We found it much easier to understand religions that are completely new and strange to us—as, for example, the religions of India and China. A greater degree of insight and of spiritual freedom is required of him who would understand the Arabian Prophet and his book.

CHAPTER I

Arabia at the Time of Mohammed

AT the time of Mohammed's appearance Arabian paganism was tending very strongly toward that type of belief which has been called polydaemonism. Divine beings, as a rule, were not such clearly defined and individual entities as in the higher polytheistic religions. They were beings after the fashion of the European fauns, gnomes, and earth-spirits, and were usually differentiated only by their different dwelling places. As in European folk-lore every home has its house-cricket, and every forest its spirit, so, according to Western Semitic belief, every country had its special divinity, a Baal or an El. The local divinity could inhabit external objects of nature, and in Semitic thought, as expressed especially in sacred stories, it could also inhabit trees or springs. In Canaan the sacred tree might be replaced by a wooden pole, an *ashera*, which was often erected near the altar. Similarly, the sacred stone might be a rocky ledge, or a single stone, which, because of its unique position, became an object of worship. Moreover, a special stone might even be erected for cult purposes. Then it was called a *masseba*. Sometimes offerings were placed upon natural boulders, or upon stones having a bowl-shaped depression, like the Nordic elf-mills. In Judges vi, 19ff, such a sacrifice is described. Gideon placed meat and unleavened bread upon a rock and poured broth over it, whereupon fire came out of the rock and consumed the offering. A large stone was generally regarded as a fitting place to offer a sacrifice. When the Ark of the Covenant was returned from the land of the Philistines, and the procession reached Bethshemesh, the Hebrews found in the field there a large stone, upon which the kine who had drawn the ark were sacrificed as a burnt-offering to the Lord.

Among the Arabs this stone cult survived and assumed a

definite form. The various local divinities, worshipped by one or more tribes of the vicinity, were ordinarily simply identified with stones—or this, at least, is the opinion of Mohammedan writers. Ibn al Kelbi reports that Manat was a large stone in the territory of the Hudhail tribe, that Allat was a rectangular stone upon which a Jew used to grind wheat, and that Sa'd was a high block of stone in the desert. In some cases the divinity was identified with a particular part of the natural rock. Al-Fals was a reddish projection, resembling a man, on an otherwise black mountain. But specially erected stones might also serve as the dwelling-places of the divinity or the seats of his power.

The most famous of all of the stone fetishes of Arabia was, of course, the black stone in the sanctuary of Mecca. The Ka'ba was, and still is, a rectangular stone structure. Built into its Eastern corner is the black stone which had been an object of worship for many centuries before Mohammed appropriated the Ka'ba for his new religion, and made the pilgrimage to this holy place one of the pillars of Islam.

Every nature cult is inclined to regard a sacred object as a personal human being. When possible, this tendency often finds expression in clumsy attempts to interpret the sacred object anthropomorphically. Hence several of the Arabian stone fetishes were in process of becoming idols. Al-Galsad looked like 'the torso of a man of white stone with a black head.' In the Ka'ba there was an actual idol representing the God Hubal.

The sacred stone image was surrounded by consecrated territory, a *Hima*, which often contained rich vegetation and a natural water-supply. In the sacred grove there was frequently a spring. Thus, on one side of the Ka'ba was the well Zemzem, whose very salty and disagreeable water is still regarded by Mohammedans as particularly holy. Within a *Hima* an animal could not be killed, nor a tree felled. Tame animals which fled into it could not be recovered, and some animals which had to be withdrawn from secular use because of ancient taboos—for example, female camels which had brought forth male colts for a number of years in succession—were placed in these sacred enclosures. As in other lands, so in Arabia, sacrifice was the method of establishing contact with the divinity. First the sinews of the hind-legs of the sacrificial animal, usually a camel, were severed, so that it fell over; thereupon its throat was cut with an archaic knife, and the blood was made to drop upon the sacred stone. The flesh was usually eaten by the sacrificer, but sometimes it was shared by guests whom he had invited to the feast. However, some sacrifices were consecrated entirely to the divinity. The sacrificial animal had then to be left lying upon the sacred place, to feed the beasts and birds of prey. Some sacrifices were prescribed by traditional customs. When a boy attained the age of seven a sheep was sacrificed, and the 'pagan hair,' *aqiqa*, of the boy was cut, from which act the whole custom, which Islam also adopted, receives its name. In offering a sacrifice a large number of taboos had to be observed until the sacrifice had been completed: such as no drinking of wine, no washing or combing, no sex contact with women, wearing nothing upon the head, and carrying no weapons.

In connection with the annual sacrifices another cult form was retained, especially at the Ka'ba. During a certain month the Arabs of the vicinity assembled to walk around the sanctuary. This circumambulation, the *tawaf*, which even to-day constitutes the climax of the Mohammedan pilgrimage, began and ended at the sacred stone, and was supposed to proceed toward the right, that is, counter sun-wise. At the beginning or at the end of the ceremony the black stone was sometimes kissed, or a bow was made with outstretched arms toward the wall between the stone and the Eastern door. This usage is obviously related to the ritual dance or the circling of the sacred object, the sacred tree, the Maypole, or the fire—the purpose apparently being to come into close contact with the power residing in the cult object, or to evoke an especially strong response from it. In addition, this sacred encircling is a very typical example of the shifting of motive which often takes place within the same magico-religious rite. That is to say, the act is performed not merely in order to obtain power from the cult object, but also in order to bind the divinity or power, to compel it or to surround it with a protective magic circle. The wall of Jericho fell when the priests marched around it; the city of Rome was protected by the sacred furrow which had been ploughed around it; and by means of the circle which was drawn three times (in the same direction as the sun) around the clearing in the wood the Norsemen bound the fire so that it might not spread into the forest. Concerning the sacrificial stone of the Laps it is said: 'The women are not permitted to encircle such sacred mountains, for fear that the God might not be confined by the circle, and might be forced to break out violently and bring some misfortune upon the women and their sex.' Originally the valley between Safa and Marwa, the two small hills north of the Ka'ba, also belonged to the *tawaf*.

Another ceremony, which was not connected with the rites of the Ka'ba before the rise of Islam, is the *Hajj*, the annual pilgrimage to 'Arafat, about two miles east of Mecca, toward Mina. This took place in a different month from the *tawaf*. Those making it gathered and waited for the signal of the leader before beginning the journey to Muzdalifa, where the night was spent in watching. Just at daybreak they all proceeded to Mina. On the way they passed three stone-heaps, upon which every participant cast a stone. At Mina an animal was sacrificed, and when the rite was completed the participants cut off their hair and put on their everyday clothes as a sign that they were now leaving the *ihram*. In the main this is still included in the pilgrimage to Mecca prescribed by Mohammed. Thus the rites of 'Arafat and Mina are so combined with it that the pilgrims must, after they have cut off their hair, go back to Mecca and perform a *tawaf*.

So the ancient paganism of Arabia may in general be regarded as an undeveloped polytheism, in which a development had just barely begun which would have gradually produced a pantheon consisting of a hierarchy of gods, formed by associating together a number of independent individual divinities. Nevertheless, some of these divinities stand out above the multitude of local deities, and reveal a more definite personal nature and a uniquely defined function. This is true, first of all, of the three goddesses of Mecca: Manat, Allat, and Al 'Uzza. Their cult was of the greatest antiquity. Judging by her name, Manat, who was especially revered by the war-like and poetic tribe of the Hudhail, south of Mecca, seems to have been a divinity of the very prevalent type of a goddess of fate and fortune. She resembles the Greek Tyche Soteira, one of the Fates, a daughter of Zeus, the liberator and helper of man on the sea, in war, and in public assemblies. As early as the days of Herodotus Allat was known as Alilat. The original form shows that her name signifies 'the Goddess.' like other ancient historians, Herodotus always sees in the gods of alien peoples the same beings whom his own people worship. The Allat of the Arabs is for him Urania. He therefore recognizes her as a goddess of heaven. Urania-Coelestis is the Graeco-Roman version of the Phoenician Astarte. This 'Carthaginian Astarte' bears also the name of the 'mother of the gods.' When the mother of the Emperor Heliogabalus, Julia Soemias, was elevated to the position of goddess of heaven (and her son to the position of sun-god) she was given the official title 'Mother of the gods, Venus Urania, Queen Juno.' But in Nabataean inscriptions the 'mother of the gods' is also called Allat. Thus we have a right to assume that in Arabic circles Allat corresponded with the great Semitic goddess of motherhood, fertility and heaven, and especially with the form which she assumed in Western Semitic regions. In Taif, where her most important sanctuary was located, she was called simply Al Rabba, 'sovereign,' a title which belonged also to Ishtar (Belit) and Astarte (Baalat). At the time of Mohammed's appearance Al 'Uzza received the most worship of the three goddesses. The name signifies 'the mighty, the honoured one,' and hence it really has much the same content as Al Rabba. In character too this goddess is very similar to Allat. Only in Northern Arabia does she seem to have retained more definitely her original connection with the planet Venus. Isaac of Antioch relates that the savage Arabs sacrificed boys and girls to the morning star, whom he also calls Al 'Uzza. He also accuses the Syrian ladies of climbing upon the roof at night and praying to the morning star to make their faces radiant with beauty. The Arab women do likewise. And yet, Isaac adds ironically, some of them are beautiful and some are ugly, just as are the women of all nations.[1] The Church Father Nilus relates that the Arabs worshipped the morning star, and on concluding a successful raid gladly sacrificed to it at dawn. Something very precious was used as a sacrifice, preferably a youth in the bloom of adolescence. In Nakhla, a few miles north of Mecca, Al 'Uzza had one of her chief sanctuaries. In the eighth year after the Hegira Mohammed sent the valiant Khalid, who later conquered Syria, with thirty horsemen to destroy this sanctuary. While Khalid was felling the last of the three sacred acacia-trees of the goddess, a naked black woman with flowing hair approached him. Her priest, who was present, cried out: 'Be courageous, Al 'Uzza, and protect thyself!' Khalid shook with terror, but took courage, and with one stroke cleft her head. Then she turned into a black cinder.[2]

How dear the bright and comely goddess of heaven was to the populace of the Mediterranean countries and the Near East is shown especially by the fact that she survived the decay of the ancient world, and won a place for herself in Catholic Christianity as the Virgin Mary, the Queen of Heaven. And the fact that Mohammed himself, who otherwise broke so completely with the old paganism, originally attempted to make a place for the three goddesses in his religious system, is reflected in a story which has been faithfully preserved by Islamic tradition, although to us it seems to present the Prophet in a very unfavourable light. Mohammed was probably actuated by a pious regard for what had been vitally religious in the piety of his childhood—something which he could not and did not desire to discard. Thanks, however, to an over-

[1] Wellhausen, Reste arabisehen Heidentums, p. 40.
[2] Wakidi (Wellhausen, *Muhammed in Medina*), p. 351.

zealous apologetic, this fact, which in itself is neither foolish nor disparaging to the Prophet, had been so portrayed, in a foolish legend, as to cast a grave reflection upon his religious and moral character.

Ibn Sa'd, an historian of the ninth century, relates[1] that at the time when Mohammed permitted some of the faithful to migrate to Abyssinia, to escape the persecution which threatened him and his followers, he strongly desired not to receive any revelations that might estrange his countrymen. He was anxious to win them, and he did succeed in reaching an understanding with them. One day he was sitting together with them at the Ka'ba, reading them Sura 53: 'By the Star when it setteth.' When he came to the passage: 'Do ye behold Allat and Al 'Uzza, and also Manat, the third idol?' —which now concludes: 'What? shall ye have male progeny and Allah female? This were indeed an unfair partition!'—Satan suggested two lines to him: 'These are the exalted females, and truly their intercession may be expected.' Mohammed then re-read the whole Sura, and at its conclusion he prostrated himself and prayed, and the whole tribe of Quraish did the same. His bitter enemy, the old Walid ibn Al-Mugira, who could not bow down, took earth instead, and sprinkled it upon his head. All were greatly pleased with the Prophet, and said to him: 'We know that Allah killeth and giveth life, createth and preserveth, but these our goddesses pray to Him for us, and since you have now permitted them to share divine honours with Him, we therefore desire to unite with you.' The Prophet was disturbed by their words, and all day he meditated alone in his own house. That evening the angel Gabriel came to him, and the Prophet recited the Sura to him. When he came to the words suggested by Satan the angel asked: 'Have I taught you these two lines?' Mohammed then realized his error, and said: 'I have attributed to Allah words which He did not reveal.'

It is very apparent that in this form the whole narrative is historically and psychologically contradictory. However,

[1] Ibn Sa'd, i, 1, p. 137.

beneath the legendary form which has come down to us there is still discernible an older version, according to which Mohammed's legitimate desire to reach an understanding with his people misled him into trying to compromise between previously proclaimed monotheism and the pagan idolatry. Inasmuch as parallels to such opportunism are by no means lacking in Mohammed's later conduct—think, for example, of his attempt to win over the Jews of Medina to his religion—this story of his chance defection has hitherto been generally accepted as historical. It is thought that in this incident the unscrupulousness of the future autocrat of Medina is clearly revealed, and it is believed that these tactics actually achieved a certain degree of success; for according to one version, although it involved only a temporary concession, which Mohammed revoked on the very same day, nevertheless, the compromise was maintained long enough for the rumour of his reconciliation with his people to reach the refugees in Abyssinia.

However, an Italian scholar, Caetani,[1] has attempted to show that the traditional form of the story cannot be correct. When one considers the contempt and enmity which the Quraish tribe, who inhabited Mecca, showed toward Mohammed on other occasions, it would seem highly improbable that they ever condescended to listen to the Prophet's reading of the Koran, to say nothing of acknowledging him as a prophet on account of an insignificant concession. Furthermore, such a sudden abandonment of a principle which he had previously championed so energetically would have utterly cancelled his previous success, and entirely undermined the prestige which he had gained among his followers. And one might add that a compromise with the Quraish tribe could not possibly have been reached by merely changing a few lines of the Koran at a time when a large portion of it was filled with bitter attacks upon the Meccan pagans and their gods.

However, in my opinion it is unthinkable that the men

[1] *Annali dell'Islam*, i, p. 278 ff.

of the later tradition, who regarded Mohammed in every respect as a perfect example for the faithful, would have deliberately invented a story so seriously compromising their Prophet. We must therefore assume, as the historical kernel of the tradition, that Sura 53, 19 ff. once embodied a different wording, implying acceptance of the pagan conception of the gods, an implication which Mohammed subsequently felt to be incompatible with belief in the one God. In style and rhythm the two Satanic lines fit admirably into the original Sura, which is amongst the earliest revelations, so that it is impossible that they should have been added as late as the Abyssinian emigration. Mohammed often made additions to the older Suras, and in such cases he always employed the formal style which dominates every revelation, so that the added lines always stand out clearly from the original. Moreover, in the original version the Sura probably contained a polemic against paganism. Mohammed objected to the expression, 'Daughters of Allah,' which his countrymen applied to the three goddesses, and declared that it was wrong to think of God as having daughters. However, he did not intend to deny that the goddesses were high heavenly beings who could make intercession to God. Such a position is really not unthinkable in the earliest period of the Prophet's career. He merely attributed to the heavenly intercessors the same position which the angels occupied in the popular religion of the Eastern Christian churches. Undoubtedly there existed at that time an actual angel cult. Didymus of Alexandria tells of countless angel chapels in the city and the countryside, to which the people made pilgrimages for the purpose of securing aid from the angels. And a Syrian priest writes concerning the archangel Michael: 'Michael is the great ruler of heavenly and earthly beings. Michael is the strong and just governor. Michael is the highest commander under the Heavenly Father. Michael lies at the feet of the Father and petitions Him: Remember Thy likeness! Michael stands before the throne of the Father and prays for the sins of men until they are forgiven."[1] And in Arabian paganism, as we shall see later, the idea of subordinate divine beings acting as mediators and intercessors is not at all unthinkable.

That Mohammed actually once thought of the three goddesses as interceding angels is shown by his later addition to the afore-mentioned Sura 53, 26-29: 'And many as are the angels in the Heavens, their intercession shall be of no avail until God hath permitted it to whomsoever He shall please, and whom He will accept. Verily it is they who believe not in the life to come, who name the angels with names of females: But herein they have no knowledge: they follow a mere conceit; and mere conceit can never take the place of truth.' Here Mohammed implies that the goddesses are in reality angels, to whom the pagans in their ignorance have given feminine names (comp. 37, 149-50: 43, 18). Albeit with strict reservations, the right of the angels to make intercession is here recognized. In regard to Mohammed's personal attitude to the goddesses of Mecca it is a peculiar and certainly a significant fact that they occupy quite a different position in his theological system to that of the male idols. In agreement with the usual Jewish and Christian conceptions he regards the male idols as evil spirits, as *jinn* to whom men have chosen to pray instead of to Allah. Besides, in a still later addition, which was evidently made subsequently in Medina, he still further clarified his monotheistic position. In it he says: 'These are mere names; ye and your fathers named them thus' (53, 23). Here the goddesses have become mere names and have no basis in reality.

It is not difficult to explain how the whole tradition of the Prophet's desire to be concilatory, and the unfortunate concession which arose from this desire, might have originated. It illustrates admirably the general character and value of most of the narratives which we possess concerning the life and the conduct of the Prophet in Mecca. When Mohammed lived in Mecca he was a comparatively insignificant man,

[1] Leipoldt, J., *Didymus der Blinde*, Texte und Untersuchungen, N.F. xiv, 3, pp. 91 ff.

and his activities assuredly did not attract the degree of attention which the later legends presuppose, so that we naturally have only a very few data relating to this period which are of any historical value. The majority of those followers who had the best understanding of the religious significance of Mohammed, and who came to realize that it was of vital interest to the faith to preserve all that was known concerning his personality, were not converted to Islam until the Medina period. Those followers who had been with the Prophet from the beginning were engaged, for the most part, as responsible leaders in the military state which was growing in power like an avalanche, and they had other things to do than relating stories of the shame and debasement of the Meccan period. Consequently those who sought information concerning that period had really only one source upon which they could depend: the Koran. In this sacred scripture, which every pious man knew by heart, they were continually confronted by allusions to particular historical situations. Since there was no one present who could give them definite information concerning the meaning of these vague references, pious imagination came to the rescue, and reconstructed the circumstances and events which were obviously implied. Thus, some interpreter of the Koran who belonged to an older generation tried to explain the tradition concerning the original wording of the 53rd Sura to a later type of piety which found it obnoxious. He found the explanation in two passages of the Koran. The first was Sura 17, 75-6: 'And, verily, they had well-nigh beguiled thee from what we revealed to thee, and caused thee to invent some other thing in our name: but in that case they would surely have taken thee as a friend; And had we not confirmed thee, thou hadst well-nigh leaned to them a little.' The context shows that these words refer to a political intrigue by means of which the Quraish had hoped to drive Mohammed out of his native city (verse 78). The other passage was Sura 22, 51, where we read, amongst other things: 'We have not sent any apostle or prophet before thee, amongst whose desires Satan hath injected not some wrong desire, but Allah shall bring to nought that which Satan hath suggested. Thus shall Allah affirm His revelations.' The wording of the tradition concerning the incorrect reading in Ibn Sa'd and Ibn Ishak, shows that it is an attempt at an exegesis, especially of the last-quoted passage from the Koran. However, this passage originated in Medina, and it is hardly likely that Mohammed still needed, ten years later, to justify himself in respect of a premature act, which he probably committed under quite different circumstances, and in the presence of entirely different witnesses. As we very well know, in Medina he was busy defending certain rather compromising modifications of his views that belong to a much later period.

However, according to the early Arabian conception of these divinities, of which only the feminine seemed to have much signifiance, and really to possess individual characteristics, there stood high over them a supreme God, the creator and ruler of the world. When Mohammed proclaimed his creed: 'There is no God but Allah,' he was not trying to introduce a new God. His pagan countrymen knew and acknowledged this divinity. His name, Allah, occurs already in pre-Mohammedan times, both in inscriptions and in compound personal names like Abd Allah, 'servant of Allah.' The effective note in Mohammed's evangelistic preaching is that he is able to accuse the pagans of acknowledging Allah as the creator of heaven and earth, and yet failing to draw the only possible conclusion from their belief; which is, to worship Allah and none else besides Him. 'If thou ask them who hath created the Heavens and the Earth, and hath imposed laws upon the sun and the moon, they will certainly say, "Allah". . If thou ask them who sendeth rain from Heaven, and by it quickeneth the earth after it hath been dead, they will certainly answer "Allah" ' (Sura 29, 61 and 63). When in extreme danger, especially on the sea, the pagans call upon Allah (29, 65; 31, 31; 17, 69), but when they are on land again, and feel safe, they share His divine honour with other beings. Allah is supposed to have given certain commandments and taboos to men (Sura 6, 139 ff.), and the most sacred oaths are sworn in His name (Sura 35, 40; 16, 40).

Thus, even though Allah was not worshipped as He deserved, the cult of Allah was not entirely neglected. A species of tithing, or offering of the first-fruits of grain and cattle, was offered to Allah as well as to the other gods (6, 137). But, above all, Allah was apparently regarded as 'the Lord of the Ka'ba,' the God to whom the cult of the highest sanctuary of Central Arabia was dedicated. In one of the oldest Suras (106) Mohammed urges his tribesmen, the Quraish, to worship 'the Lord of this house, who allows the two annual trade caravans to be equipped, and who cares for them, and permits them to dwell in security. Concerning himself he says that he has received the commandment to worship 'the Lord of the house,' i.e. the Ka'ba. Apparently, then, the Prophet and his countrymen fully agree that the God who is worshipped through the ritual of the Ka'ba is Allah. Since the Arabic-speaking Jews and Christians also used Allah as the name for the one God of their monotheistic belief, it so happened that the Christian Arabs, at least, regarded the Christian God as the Lord of the Ka'ba, and in consequence they occasionally participated in the cult which was celebrated there. In one oath the Christian poet Adi Ibn Zeid mentions 'Mecca's Lord and the Crucified' together.[1]

The question has been asked: How could a religion such as the ancient Arabian, which was otherwise so inadequate and under-developed, attain to so lofty a conception of God as is expressed in the belief in Allah? Wellhausen in his day tried to explain this as being an effect of the power of language over thought.[2] Allah is a contraction of *al-ilah;* and the name denotes simply 'the God.' Every tribe called its local divinity by this name. Being the only god worshipped by the members of the tribe, he did not need to be called by his name, if he possessed one. And since every tribe spoke of 'the god,' and meant thereby its own tribal god, this

[1] Cheikho, L., *ash-Shu'ara' an-nasraniyya*, Beirut, 1890, p. 451.
[2] Wellhausen, *Reste arabischen Heidentums*, pp. 218 ff.

linguistic form eventually paved the way for the belief in a supreme God common to all the tribes. This explanation of Wellhausen's is based upon a method of reasoning which several decades ago seemed very modern and scientific, especially in the type of religious research which was dominated by the standpoint of philology. To-day one would hardly credit language with such tremendous significance as a creative factor in the development of ideas. And a more profound investigation, especially of primitive religion, shows that the problem of the origins of religious conceptions is not so simple as this and other similar linguistic explanations would assume. Then, too, Allah has attributes which are certainly not shared by any local tribal gods; in especial His attribute of creator of the whole world.

It is perhaps more probable that the pagan Arabs were influenced by the many Jewish immigrants who had lived among them for centuries, especially in Yemen, but also in the central and north-western portions of the peninsula, and that their world of religious ideas owed much to the impressions which they had received from these Jews, and from the monotheistic belief of the neighbouring Christian peoples. However, among many peoples, and even among such as live at a much lower level of culture than the Bedouin of Mohammed's day, one may find a belief in a supreme god Who is the creator of the world and of men; a god Who instituted sacred customs and ceremonies, and watches over them, and especially over those removed from the control of human authority, to ensure they are maintained. It is characteristic of such gods that they recede into the background of the cult, and are but rarely called upon; for example, in times of threatening danger, or when grave natural calamities menace the existence of the social organism. Formerly scholars were generally inclined to regard this belief in a supreme God, which has been designated by the very inappropriate name of 'primitive monotheism,' as being due to the influence exerted in the course of the centuries by Christian missionaries upon primitive peoples. To-day, however, as a result of the investigations of W. Schmidt, Preuss, Pettazoni, and others, the opinion is gaining ground among scholars that this explanation no longer suffices to explain all cases, and that we must rather assume that we are here dealing with an original conception of a very ancient type. For we find it, in a pronounced form, even among those peoples who are at the most primitive level of culture. Thus it is actually possible that the belief in Allah, the creator of the world, the giver of rain, the founder of sacred customs, and the Mighty One who watches over the sacredness of oaths, is part of the autochthonous religion of Arabia. When the other deities are at times regarded as only a kind of mediator between men and Allah (39, 4), or are placed in subjection to Him as His children (39, 6), such conceptions find striking correspondences among primitive peoples today. The Safwa, in what was formerly German East Africa, explain that, just as the unimportant man who wants to bring a matter to the attention of the chief needs an important person to act as his mediator and advocator, so such a person is necessary when approaching Nguruve (God). 'The ancestors are our advocates; they can bring our affairs before God, the great Lord.'[1] And among the Ewe-speaking peoples of South Togoland the Trowo are called the 'earth gods,' but also 'Mawu's (God's) children.' 'They can bring the affairs of men before God.'[2]

At any rate, it is clear that this belief was of very great importance for Mohammed, and that in many respects his conduct cannot be understood until we remember that belief in the God whose will and plans he desired to proclaim may be regarded as being, in a certain sense, known and recognized even among the pagans. As we shall see later, this explains why Mohammed was able to begin his preaching, in an extremely abrupt and unsystematic fashion, with the proclamation of the Resurrection and the Judgment, without first clearly establishing the fundamental tenets upon which he desired to build, and without laying down a definite pro-

[1] Kootz-Kretschmer, Elise, *The Safwa*, 1926, i, p. 236.
[2] Spieth, J., *Die Religion der Eweer in Südtogo*, 1911, p. 37.

gramme of worship and religious custom. In fact, he did not at first intend to establish a new religion, but rather to reform the belief in Allah which already existed, and to show what this belief truly signified and rightfully demanded. Only gradually did the consequences of his own faith become clear to him. But it became increasingly evident that the God of judgment and of just retribution could not tolerate that other beings should receive the slightest portion of the divine honours which were His due. The strictness of Mohammed's monotheistic attitude became increasingly severe. He went much farther than Eastern Christianity, whose Christolatry and Mariolatry he regarded as idolatry. Not even Judaism withstood the test of his monotheistic zeal. He regarded the Jewish reverence for Ezra as on the same level as the Christian adoration of Jesus (9, 30).

So we can understand how it happened that Mohammed, in his early career, found himself fundamentally at one with his people, and how their national sanctuary, to which he clung with his whole heart, always remained a holy place to him. From this point of view we can also understand why at first he should even have tried to find a way of reconciling a sort of veneration of the Meccan goddesses with the new belief in eternal life which he proclaimed. His own inner development, the deepening of his own spiritual life, led him gradually to a radical break with the religion of his people.

The fact that Jews and Christians also acknowledged Allah as the only true God is likewise significant in interpreting Mohammed's conception of the relationship of the religions to one another. That all nations, even though with greater or less purity, or with varying degrees of whole-heartedness, worship the same God, and therefore must at various times have had a knowledge of His will, became the natural presupposition of the doctrine of revelation which Mohammed developed, prompted by influences whose origin we shall seek to establish later.

A special priesthood guarded and directed the Arabian sanctuaries. The priest or temple guard (the Arabic *sadin*) was, like the Nordic *Gode*, a venerable man who was regarded as the owner of the sacred precinct. As a rule this privilege of ownership and direction belonged to a clan whose chief was the actual priest, but any members of the tribe could carry out the priestly functions, which, in addition to the guarding of the sacred grove and the building (when such existed), or the image of the God, and the treasury where the votive gifts were stored, consisted merely of the practice of casting lots to determine the will of God, or to obtain His advice concerning important undertakings. However, for the sacrifice itself no priest was necessary. Every head of a family could sacrifice for himself and his family.

In addition to the priesthood, there was a certain guild of seers whose members received their esoteric knowledge from a spirit, a *jinni*, or, as Mohammed described it in less friendly terms, from Satan. It was said that the seer, *kahin*, was *majnun*, that is, possessed by a *jinni*. But in Mohammed's day we find that the relation of the seer to the spirit is no longer thought of as possession. It is a personal fellowship, in which the *jinni* tells his friend what he knows. According to Mohammed's conception a *jinni* attempts to get hold of what has been transacted among the heavenly beings, and what has been written upon the heavenly tablets, and then 'cackles it into the ear of his friend as a hen cackles.' But when the Koran was revealed to Mohammed angels were stationed to guard heaven, and whenever they discovered one of these *jinn* listening they hurled a flaming meteor at him and killed him. And like the seer, the poet also was inspired by a spirit, a *jinni*. At the beginning of his career a poet occasionally met his Muse, who used physical force to make him the poet of his tribe. One day Hassan Ibn Thabit was walking through a street in Medina. A female spirit pressed him down, kneeling upon his chest, and said: 'Are you the man whom your people expect to become their poet?' Then she forced him to utter three verses, and Hassan, who had never been able to compose before, became a poet. He was in the real sense 'Musoleptos,' possessed by the Muse.

A *kahin* was asked for advice about important undertakings, lost articles, and stray camels. The reply of the oracle was given in a sort of rhymed prose, *saj'*, often intentionally obscure and twisted. Mohammed's inspiration must have reminded his countrymen of the seers. An accusation which he was frequently forced to hear from the pagans of Mecca was that he was *majnun*, that he had a *jinni* who gave him his revelations. Mohammed was deeply hurt by this accusation. But he does not dispute the formal justification of the comparison. However, he seeks to emphasize the fact that the being who came to him was no ordinary mean divining spirit, but a lofty and heavenly being, one near the throne of the Lord (Sura 53). Consequently his message is of a higher value than the half-true sayings of *jinn* concerning future events. Apart from the external similarity of the conception of inspiration—just as Gabriel reads the Koran to the prophet, so the *jinni* whispers the desired oracle to his friend—Mohammed, at least unconsciously, absorbed impressions from the pagan soothsayers. For example, many *kahins* were wont to cover their heads when they wished to evoke a revelation. Mohammed did likewise (Sura 73, 1; 74, 1). The *velatio* was a proven method of producing inspiration. Thus the Druid wrapped himself in the hide of the sacrificed ox, and the Icelandic seer in a grey sheepskin. Among the poets, Milton and Bousset knew how to stimulate an artistic inspiration.[1] The oldest Suras of the Koran begin with a formal incantation, in which natural objects or mystical beings and powers are invoked. 'By heaven and the Zodiac and the prophesied day and the witness and the accused.' 'By the dawn and the ten nights, by the plain and the mountains and the night when it vanishes.' That is the mysterious oracular style of the *kahins*, and in this style they introduced their *saj'* poems.

[1] Andrae, T., *Mystikens psykologi*, 1926, p. 615.

CHAPTER II

From Mohammed's Childhood to His Prophetic Call

OUR earliest Gospel (Mark) begins with the baptism of Jesus at the Jordan, and his consecration to the office of the Messiah. The authentic history of Mohammed begins in like fashion with his appearance as a prophet in Mecca. What is related of his earlier experiences is mainly legendary. If I do not here completely ignore these pious legends, which otherwise belong more properly to the history of the beliefs of his followers than to the biography of the Prophet, my reason is that it is important, merely from the historical point of view, to become acquainted with the great personalities of the world religions dressed in those garments in which the pious faith of their followers have clothed them. The manger of Bethlehem and the song of the angels belong to the portrait of Jesus, and the fourfold contact with suffering and the renunciation of the pleasures of the palace to the portrait of Buddha. Something of the magic of their personalities, which we might not understand in any other way, speaks to us through the poetry of faith.

We do not know definitely when Mohammed was born. One tradition asserts that his birth occurred in the 'elephant year.' This refers to the oft-mentioned campaign which the Ethiopian viceroy in Yemen, Abraha, undertook about A.D. 560 in the interior of Arabia. But according to Procopius this war was really directed against Persia, and formed a part of the great war which the Emperor Justinian fought between 540 and 562 with Khosroes I Anushirwan. So it must have taken place before 562. Abraha's expedition, which was actually undertaken upon the instigation of the Byzantine Emperor, and which aimed at attacking the Persian power by land, received a religious motive in Arabian tradition. When Abraha saw that the Arabs were making their way to Allah's house in Mecca in droves at the time of the pilgrimage, he asked: 'Of what is this house made?' and received the answer: 'Of stone, dressed with striped material from Yemen.' Then he said: 'By Messiah! I will truly build you a better house!' He then built a church in Sana'a out of white, red, green, and black marble, the doors being covered with gold and studded with pearls and precious stones, and he caused incense to be burned within, and the walls to be sprinkled with musk, and then he told the people to make their pilgrimages to the temple. But when an Arab desecrated the sanctuary in a despicable fashion, Abraha became angry and swore to tear down the Ka'ba in punishment. So he wrote to the king of Abyssinia and requested him to send his elephant Mahmud, the largest and strongest elephant in the world. With this elephant and a mighty army he began the march to Mecca. But when the army came to the sacred environs of the temple, a flock of birds flew from the sea, and every bird had one stone in its beak and one in each claw. They dropped these stones upon Abraha's army, and wherever a stone fell it caused an eruption as in smallpox. The elephant dared not enter the sacred territory, but retreated in terror. King Abraha himself died a painful death, one member of his body after another dropping off.[1] Mohammed alludes to Abraha's campaign in Sura 105, in which the legend of the birds is related. This is of interest to us, inasmuch as it proves that Mohammed originally shared the political sympathies of his people. Later, after he had broken decisively with his people, he made an alliance with the hated Abyssinians.

However, the statement that Mohammed was born in the 'elephant year' does not agree with other chronological facts in the life of the Prophet. According to a tradition which is often repeated in the earliest records of Islam, he received the prophetic call at the age of forty, thirteen years before his migration to Medina. Reckoning from this, then, Mohammed must have been born in the year 569, and he would have received his call in 609. On the other hand, there is complete

[1] Ibn Sa'd, i, 1, pp. 55 ff.

agreement concerning the date of his emigration, 622, and the date of his death ten years later, in 632. The fixed point in the earliest Mohammedan chronology is the Hegira, the emigration of the Prophet from Mecca. As early as the time of the Caliph Omar—that is, not later than 644—the faithful begin to reckon the years according to this event, or more correctly, according to the beginning of the year in which it occurred. The new era, then, began on July 15, 622, but Mohammed's Hegira did not occur until September 25th of that year. The Mohammedan year is a lunar year, consisting of six months of twenty-nine days and six months of thirty days. Thus the entire year has 354 days. In every thirty years there are eleven leap years of 355 days. Therefore the Mohammedan years shift continually in relation to the Christian, the discrepancy amounting to a little over three years in a century. On May 19, 1931, the year 1350 of the Mohammedan era began.

According to orthodox tradition the Prophet came from a family of very high rank. When Allah wishes to select a prophet He chooses first the best tribe, and then the best man. Allah surveyed the human families from their first beginnings and chose the best of every branch, until He finally came to the tribe Banu Kinana, in which He settled upon the subdivision Quraish, and from the Quraish He chose the family Banu Hashim. According to legend Hashim was a prominent man. He had equipped the two annual caravans to Yemen and Syria, and was on good terms with the Negus as well as with the emperor. His son Abd al Muttalib was the grandfather of the Prophet, in whose house Mohammed was reared. According to a Shiite legend,[1] the future greatness of his grandson was revealed to him in a wondrous vision. In a dream he saw growing out of his back a tree whose top reached to the sky and whose branches stretched out toward the East and the West. A light seven times brighter than the sun emanated from it, and Persians as well as Arabs worshipped it. A soothsayer, to whom he related this dream, declared that

[1] Al-Qummi, *Kitab Ramal al-din*, Teheran, 1300, p. 103.

from among his descendants a man would arise who would become a world-ruler and a prophet of humanity. If, then, we can accept the statement of the chroniclers of Islam, Abd al Muttalib was 'a prominent man, a man who commanded obedience, a ruler among his people.' It was his function to apportion the water from the well Zemzem to the pilgrims, and to supervise the feeding of them. He it was who, through a dream-revelation, rediscovered the well Zemzem. Legend has it that Allah once made the well spring forth for Ishmael, the tribal ancestor of the Arabs. His mother Hagar had come to Mecca while wandering about in the desert. When her son was on the point of dying of thirst she first ascended Safa, and then Marwa, to beg help of Allah. Then Allah sent Gabriel to the lad. He struck the ground with his foot so that water began to trickle upwards. This was the origin of the well of Zemzem. Abd al Muttalib had ten sons: 'Among the Arabs there were no more prominent and stately men, none of more noble profile. Their noses were so large that the nose drank before the lips.'[1] Abd al Muttalib's son Abdallah, the father of the Prophet, married Amina Bint Wahb. Shortly after this marriage Abdallah died in Medina while on a trip to Syria. He left to his widow and their unborn child only an old female slave and five camels.

Even while Amina was carrying Mohammed in her womb remarkable signs occurred which foretold his future greatness. The mother experienced none of the burdens of pregnancy, and was unconscious of her condition until one day, in a state midway between sleep and waking, she heard a voice which said: 'The son whom you are to bear shall be the ruler and prophet of his people.' After a time she heard the voice again: 'Seek refuge in the Only One, the Eternal, against the malice of envious people.' When she told this to her female relatives they advised her to wear iron rings around her neck and arms. She did so, but after a few days she found that the rings were broken, so she ceased to wear them. Finally the voice was heard a third time commanding her to

[1] Ibn Sa'd, i, 1, p. 57.

name the child Ahmad. According to Sura 61, 6, Jesus foretold Mohammed's coming, when he mentioned 'an apostle that shall come after me whose name shall be Ahmad!' Ahmad has the same significance as Mohammed—'the illustrious.' It is usually assumed that some Arabic Christian, who knew Greek, played upon the words of Jesus in the Gospel of John, where he promises his disciples to send them another comforter. Instead of *parakletos* he reads *periklytos*, which signifies Ahmad in Arabic.[1]

Concerning Mohammed's birth miraculous things are related, such as were told earlier concerning the births of Moses, Buddha, Alexander, Jesus, Mary, and many others. In the hour of his birth a brilliant light shone over the entire world from East to West. With miraculous clairvoyance Amina saw the palaces of Syria and the necks of the camels in Busrah. When Mohammed was born he fell to the ground, took a handful of earth, and gazed toward heaven. He was born clean and without a spot, as a lamb is born, circumcized, and with the navel-cord already cut.

The birth of the Prophet did not escape the notice of the initiated. The Jews, who had their sacred scriptures, knew of it, and the seers, who received news from their spirits. Hassan ibn Thabit is said to have declared: 'I was a boy of seven or eight years of age when I heard a Jew speaking in the streets of Medina in a loud voice, calling his countrymen. When they had all assembled he said: "To-night the star of Ahmad, which proclaims his birth, has arisen." '[2]

The legend of the young hero who grew up among the shepherds has also been associated with the Prophet of Islam. It states that shortly after his birth he was entrusted to the care of a family belonging to the Bedouin tribe of Banu Sa'd ibn Bakr. Halimah, his foster-mother, accepted the fatherless boy without charge. But she noticed that from that very hour a blessing rested upon her home. One day, when Mohammed

[1] Pautz, *Muhammed's Lehre von der Offenbarung*, p. 126.
[2] Ibn Hisham, Sira (on the margin of Ibn Qayyim al-Jauziyya, *Zad al-ma'ad*, Cairo, 1324) i, p. 87.

was four years old, he and his little foster-brothers were with the sheep, at some distance from the tent. Two angels came to him and laid him upon the ground. Then they opened his body, took a black drop from his heart, and washed his inward parts with melted snow from a golden vessel. Thereupon they weighed him, first against ten, then against a hundred, and finally against a thousand people of his nation; but he tipped the scale. Then one of the angels said: 'Stop! For even if you weigh him against his whole nation he will weigh more.' A similar treatment is undergone by future medicine-men and ghost-seers among various peoples. Australian sorcerers say that a spirit seizes them, cuts open their hearts, and places a rock-crystal inside, which gives them the faculty of clairvoyance.

When the boy was five years of age Halimah wished to take him back to his mother. When she came to the heights before Mecca she realized that he was lost. When he was found, after a long search, his grandfather Abd al Muttalib took him upon his shoulders, carried him around the Ka'ba, and prayed for him.

At the age of six the fatherless boy lost his mother also. It was said that she was such a good woman that the *jinn* wept at her death. It is related that when nearing the end of his life, after the Prophet had conquered Mecca, he was seen to thrown himself upon a dilapidated grave. The people sat down around him. For a moment it seemed as if he intended to speak. But he remained silent, and finally arose, weeping. Umar, who of all his followers was least afraid in the presence of the Prophet, asked him why he wept. Mohammed replied: 'This is the grave of my mother. I have asked permission of Allah to visit it, and He has granted my request. Then I asked Him for forgiveness for my mother, but He would not hear me. Therefore I am weeping.'[1] Later, when Mohammed had become much more than a human intercessor and mediator for his people, the idea that his parents should be subject to eternal punishment, like pagans, seemed in-

[1] Ibn Sa'd, i, 1, p. 84.

tolerable. So a later legend states that Allah in His mercy awakened Mohammed's father and mother from death for a while so their son might convert them to the true faith.[1]

The fatherless and motherless boy found a home with his grandfather Abd al Muttalib, who loved him more than his own children. But after two years the grand-father died, and Mohammed went to his uncle, whose real name was Abd Manaf, but who was usually called by his *'kunya'* (the honorary name which an Arab accepts when a son is born to him), Abu Talib, 'Talib's father.' It is said also of Abu Talib that he loved Mohammed greatly. He would not sleep unless the lad were at his side, and he never cared to go out without him. He noticed also that a blessing accompanied the future prophet. When Mohammed was not present Abu Talib's family could not eat. And from other signs it was evident that Mohammed was no ordinary child. Other children had watery eyes and scrubby hair. But he always looked as if he had been anointed and treated with eye-salve.[2]

When Mohammed was twelve years old his uncle was compelled to go to Syria with a trade caravan, and since he did not wish to be separated from his nephew he took the boy along with him. Now in Bostra, in Syria, there was a monk named Buhaira, who possessed all the esoteric knowledge of the Christians. Monk after monk had lived in the hermit's cell where Buhaira dwelt, and each monk had bequeathed his knowledge to his successor, and this knowledge was also recorded in a book which was in the cell. The caravans of the Quraish had often passed the monk's cell, but he had never paid the slightest attention to them. But this time, to their great astonishment, he invited the whole caravan young and old, slave and freeman, to a feast. Mohammed was considered too young to be taken to the feast, but Buhaira inquired especially for him, and would not be satisfied until he had been brought. The reason for this was that Buhaira

[1] Nabhani, *Al-anwar al-muhammadiyya min al-mawahib al-laduniyya*, Cairo, 1320, p. 22.

[2] Ibn Sa'd, i, 1, p. 76.

had seen how a cloud shaded Mohammed as he was riding in the caravan, and how a tree had lowered its branches over him to give him shade at the resting-place. When Mohammed arrived the monk examined him carefully, and found on him the signs which were known to him in accordance with the secret knowledge which was contained in the book. Between his shoulders he found the seal of the prophetic office. He also questioned Mohammed carefully concerning many things, and especially concerning his dreams, and he discovered that all was correct. Then he took Abu Talib aside, and said to him: 'Return to your country with your nephew, and guard him against the Jews, for if they see him, and know what I know concerning him, they will seek to do him harm.'[1]

The statement that Mohammed as a youth visited Syria, in the company of his uncle and in the service of his future wife, has been accepted as historical fact by many writers, and it has been thought that the impressions which he there received of the customs and rites of the Christians provided the first stimulus to his religious reform. As we shall learn, Mohammed did know a great deal about Christianity. But he did not gain his knowledge by direct contact. His naïve conception of the religion of the Bible, which he regarded as agreeing absolutely with his own religion, the absence of all allusions to conditions which he would have noticed had he ever really visited a Christian country, or been in a church, or witnessed a procession—all this proves that we can hardly assume that Mohammed ever visited Christian Syria. There is a distinct difference to be observed between him and the widely travelled pagan or nominally Christian poets of his age. In their poetry we find frequent allusions to the various external trappings of the Christian cult, which would naturally impress the stranger from pagan Arabia. But the spirit and teaching of Christianity are absolutely alien to them. Mohammed, on the other hand, betrays in some respects a surprising lack of knowledge concerning the forms of the Christian cult. To the climax of the service, the Lord's Supper,

[1] Ibn Sa'd, i, 1, p. 99.

he refers only once, and that in a manner which shows that he conceives of it as an actual meal. 'Jesus, Son of Mary said—"O God, our Lord! send down a table to us out of Heaven, that it may become a recurring festival to us, to the first of us and to the last of us, and a sign from thee; and do thou nourish us . . ."' (5, 114). This is Mohammed's conception of the institution of the Lord's Supper. Probably a liturgical expression concerning the heavenly bread, the nourishment for the soul, stimulated his imagination. His contemporary, the poet A'sha, who had been at the Christian court in Hira, speaks differently when he sings in a drinking-song of the red wine which 'the monk carries in the procession, setting it down and standing before it longingly, praying over the goblet.'[1] In Mohammed's sayings concerning Christianity all traces of such personal observation are lacking. On the other hand, he shows a deeper understanding of the spirit of Oriental Christianity than his contemporaries. Our only authentic source, the Koran, shows us very clearly the figure of a seeker and dreamer who fashions his conceptions according to the information which comes to him by chance rather than derived from concrete and living realities. The wonderful experience of inspiration makes this self-created picture in the soul of the Prophet more vivid than any image of reality, and for him it is and remains the only correct picture, in spite of all contradictions.

That Abu Talib proved to be a loyal kinsman of Mohammed is shown by the fact that when the persecution of the Prophet began he, as well as the rest of the family, defended him and refused to deliver him to his enemies. Whether his motive was merely family pride, or whether a personal attachment bound the uncle to Mohammed, cannot be decided. The fact remains that Abu Talib never embraced Islam. He did not die until three years before the Hegira. A legend states that when Abu Talib was near death Mohammed went to him and tried to persuade him to confess the faith of Islam. But

[1] Cheikho, L., *An-Nasraniyya wa-adabuha bain'Arab al-Jahiliyya*, Beirut, 1912, p. 39.

two of Mohammed's bitterest enemies had previously visited the sick man, and one of them, Abu Lahab, said: 'Will you desert the faith of your fathers?' The dying man answered: 'I hold to the faith of Abd al Muttalib.' These were his last words. When he was dead Mohammed locked himself in his house for several days to pray for his soul. But he ceased when Gabriel came to him with Sura 9, 114: 'It is not for the prophet or the faithful to pray for the forgiveness of those, even though they be of kin, who associate other beings with God.'[1] It might be supposed that the grave dogmatic problem, whether there is a justification for praying for relatives who have died in unbelief, would be solved by such a definite statement. But in Islam also there is an art of theological exegesis which can make the impossible seem possible. Scribes of the Basra school claim that the words really mean: 'It is not for the prophet to pray for forgiveness'—namely, 'in so far as Allah does not grant him permission.' In this way the door is left open to those who espouse a more liberal view of the question.[2]

When Mohammed was twenty-five years of age his uncle said to him one day: 'I am a poor man, and the times are hard for us. Khadijah is sending a caravan to Syria. You ought to go and offer your services to her.' Khadijah was the widow of a merchant, an energetic and resolute woman, the noblest, most distinguished, and richest among the Quraish. Khadijah gladly accepted Mohammed's offer, and gave him double wages; that is, four camels instead of two. On the way to Syria the incident occurred which we have already described. The monk who was then inhabiting the cell was called Nestur. Mohammed gained such influence over the caravan that even its leader seemed to be his slave; their business was highly successful, and the profit was twice as great as usual. When the caravan returned to Mecca, Khadijah, sitting in her high seat, observed how Mohammed was being shaded by two angels as he rode upon his donkey. After a time she

[1] Ibn Sa'd, i, 1, p. 78.
[2] Tabari, Tafsir to 9, 114.

sent a message to Mohammed asking him if he had no intention of marrying. When he made the excuse of poverty the messenger said: 'But if I tell you of a match where you may gain beauty, wealth, and noble birth?' When Mohammed learned that Khadijah herself was offering her hand to him he accepted at once. It is said that Khadijah made her father drunk with wine, since she did not expect to gain his consent in any other way. When he became sober he found that he had already been clothed in the garment with which, according to ancient custom, the son-in-law honoured his father-in-law at the wedding. Mohammed was twenty-five at this time, and Khadijah forty.[1]

Khadijah seems really to deserve the reputation which tradition has given her. When Mohammed began his career as a prophet she stood loyally by him. That the marriage was a happy one may be inferred from the fact that Mohammed, who in later years gradually increased the number of his wives to nine, took no other women as long as she lived. 'Ayesha, his pampered favourite, once dared to say, when Mohammed was speaking of Khadijah: 'Allah has given you one who is better than she,' referring to herself. But the Prophet replied gravely: 'No, no one is better than Khadijah. She believed in me when all others were unbelieving; she took my words to be true when all others treated me as a liar.'[2]

Not much of what tradition tells us of the life of the Prophet before his call is authentic. Only this is certain, that he belonged to a respected but not wealthy family, that he lost his father early in life, and grew up in a poor home, but that he later gained economic independence through his marriage. In one of his earliest revelations he reflects upon the mercy which God has shown him in previous years. 'Did He not find thee an orphan and give thee a home? And find thee erring and guide thee, and find thee needy and enrich thee?' (Sura 93, 6-8). When the attempt is made to explain the bitter attacks which Mohammed made upon the

[1] Ibn Sa'd, i, 1, pp. 89 ff.
[2] *Nabhani*, p. 96.

unmerciful rich as being due to his bitter experiences as a poor orphan, it should not be forgotten that precisely in those years when his call came to him he himself was wealthy, and that Abu Talib's family, even though they were poor, would under no circumstances have expected or accepted charity. By means of self-help within the family they were secure against privation. The warning against greed, worldliness, and hard-heartedness originates, as we shall see, from another source than that of personal experience.

So the year approached when the time was ripe for Islam. Mohammed was now forty years old, an independent and, it seems, a respected man. It is said that among his countrymen he was known by the epithet Al-Amin, 'the reliable,' and even if this designation does not seem to express the most apparent trait of Mohammed's character, it does show that he had an unusual power of inspiring confidence. The records do not tell us with certainty what his occupation was. That he was a merchant is only an assumption, based upon the fact that he married the widow of a merchant, and has employed certain commercial expressions and terms in the Koran. But we have no definite statements to the effect that Mohammed ever undertook commercial journeys for his wife or for himself, and the commercial expressions actually belong to the religious terminology which Mohammed accepted. They were not invented.

As the time drew near when Allah desired to make Mohammed His prophet, the holy element and its approach first became noticeable in his dreams. He had visions as bright as the dawn. He came to love solitude. He wandered upon mountain paths and in ravines far from the city. Even the stones and trees greeted him with the salutation: 'Peace be with thee, Allah's Apostle.' He often looked to see, but was unable to discover who called him. Once each year he retired to a cave on Mount Hira for a month, where he spent the time in devotional practices.

The call of the invisible draws man into silence and solitude. Even savage seers and prophets love to sojourn in the forest, or upon the mountains, and there await the call of the spirit. But the solitary devotions in the cave of Mount Hira remind us rather of the ascetic practices of Syrian Christianity. Syrian piety was dominated by the ideal of monastic religion. Even the pious laymen loved to retire into solitude at times, in order to live, at least for a while, the perfect life of the hermit. Examples are not lacking to show that pagans also adopted the same practice. It is said of Bishop Habel of Arbela that while he was still a pagan he often deserted the sheep which he tended and 'Sat down in a cave and became absorbed in reflections upon the vanity and nothingness of this world.'[1]

All inspired men regard the first time of hearing the voice of inspiration as an occasion of the greatest moment. No matter how many other facts are omitted, the story of this fundamental experience is never lacking in their biographies, and often it is the fixed point in their spiritual life, to which they constantly return, especially in times of doubt and uncertainty concerning the validity of their call. In the vision which usually follows the call the hidden striving and longing of the soul find concrete expression. As if by a formula, it often reproduces the innermost tendency of the personality.

In the earliest of our authorities, Ibn Ishak (d. 768), the story of Mohammed's call reads:[2] 'In the year that Mohammed was called to be a prophet he went to Mt. Hira with his family in the month of Ramadan in order to devote himself to solitary religious exercises. "One night," the Prophet states, "Gabriel came to me with a cloth as I slept and said: Recite! I answered: I cannot recite! So he choked me with the cloth until I believed that I should die. Then he released me and said: Recite (*Iqra*)!" The Prophet hesitated, and twice again the angel repeated the harsh treatment. Then finally Mohammed asked: "What shall I recite?" The angel said: Recite thou, in the name of the Lord who created—

[1] Sachau, *Die Chronik von Arbela*, Abh. der Preuse. Ak. der Wiss., 1915, Phil.-hist. Kl. 6, p. 55. Comp. T. Andrae, *Der Ursprung des Islams und das Christentum*, Kyrkohistorisk Arsskrift, 1923-25, 1925, p. 93.

[2] Ibn Hisham, p. 126.

Who created man from clots of blood. Recite thou! For thy Lord is the most beneficent, who hath taught the use of the pen—hath taught man what he knoweth not (Sura 96, 1-4). "I awoke," said Mohammed, "from my sleep, and it was as if they had written a message in my heart. I went out of the cave, and while I was on the mountain, I heard a voice saying: O Mohammed, thou art Allah's Apostle, and I am Gabriel! I looked up and saw Gabriel in the form of a man with crossed legs at the horizon of heaven. I remained standing and observed him, and moved neither backwards nor forwards. And when I turned my gaze from him, I continued to see him on the horizon, no matter where I turned." Finally the vision vanished, and Mohammed returned to his family.'

The earliest biographers of the Prophet found most of their material, especially that which referred to the period before the Hegira, in the longer, connected descriptions especially suited for recitation by popular narrators. Hence their scientific labours were devoted chiefly to the task of separating the pious narratives into the various separate accounts from which they had been compiled. In spite of his notable attempts Ibn Ishak did not entirely succeed in carrying out this critical sifting of the material.[1]

However, Ibn Sa'd,[2] a historian of the ninth century who compiled a tremendous biographical encyclopaedia relating to the Prophet and his followers and their successors, tells a story of Mohammed's call which contains only the vision of the angel on the horizon. However, a somewhat later authority, Bukhari,[3] who compiled a collection of 'traditions,' or alleged sayings of the Prophet, which have become practically canonical in the eyes of Mohammedans, tells only the story of the angel who commanded the Prophet to recite, and brings in the vision upon the mountain in a different connection as a later revelation. So Ibn Ishak, or his source, actually combined two different narratives of the call of the

[1] Fück, H., *Muhammed Ibn Ishaq*, Frankfurt a. M., 1925, p. 93.
[2] Ibn Sa'd, i, 1, p. 129 ff.
[3] Bukhari, *K. bad' al-wahi, K. tafsir* (Sura 74).

Prophet. Both of them cannot be true, or at least they cannot both constitute the call-vision of the Prophet.[1] For the two stories are of quite different character. One of them is a nocturnal vision occurring in a dark cave, while the other is a vision which the Prophet received in clear daylight, out on the open mountain.

Hitherto Western biographers have generally accepted the story of the angel who forced the Prophet to recite as the original and genuine description of the Prophet's call. In so doing they have followed the conception which is so widespread among Mohammedan authorities, and which is determined by the version of Bukhari, given in his well-known work on the traditions. Considered from the psychological standpoint, of course, the experience in the cave on Mt. Hira seems plausible enough. The conception of a spirit which literally pounces upon the inspired man, throwing him to the ground and conquering his human obstinacy, is found among various peoples. The Arabian poet was thrown to the ground by a *jinni* who kneeled upon his chest; the Greek poet was *musoleptos*, that is, possessed by the goddess of song; and the prophet of Israel felt the hand of Yahweh resting heavily upon him. In West Africa and Melanesia the strong convulsions of prospective priests or sorcerers were taken as proof of their possession by a spirit. Even in recent revival movements we hear of the obvious manipulations of the spirit. When Finney preached in Rochester in 1830 his listeners quickly fell to the ground all around him. 'I could not have cut them down any faster if I had had a sword in my hand.' And in fact this peculiar complex of bodily symptoms may be described, for want of a better name, as a hysterical attack, and such symptoms may occur also in certain states of violent psychic tension or excitement. To the bystander the attack appears as a falling to the ground, where the victim writhes in cramps, as if he were struck down by an invisible hand. But the victim himself experiences the spell as a literal attack,

[1] For this whole problem comp. T. Andrae, *Die Legenden von der Berufung Muhammeds*, Le Monde Oriental, vi, 1912, pp. 5—18.

in which something frequently chokes and crushes him like a demon. At times he imagines that his body is being cut to pieces or pierced. Saint Theresa believed that an angel pierced her body with a golden spear. An Australian sorcerer will tell how the spirit is cutting the body open.

Now did Mohammed really experience his call in this fashion? If he did, then, as far as I know, the Prophet of Islam is the only one among the inspired who has written an entire and comprehensive book of revelations without once referring his revelations to, or even mentioning, the experience which first gave him the certainty of his vocation. For in the Koran there is not the slightest reference to a vision such as that beheld in the cave of Mt. Hira. In order to combat the statement that he was possessed by a *jinni,* or spirit, Mohammed refers in two different places to an appearance in which he himself saw that being whose voice had spoken Allah's words into his ear or his heart. In Sura 53 he describes this vision as follows: 'By the star when it setteth, your compatriot erreth not, nor is he led astray, neither speaketh he from mere impulse. This is no other than a revelation revealed to him. One terrible in power taught it to him, endued with wisdom. With even balance stood He in the highest part of the horizon. Then He came nearer and approached, and was at the distance of two bows, or even closer—and He revealed to His servant what He revealed.' A brief description of the same vision is found in Sura 81, 19. 'That this is the word of an illustrous Messenger, endued with power, having influence with the Lord of the Throne, obeyed there by Angels, faithful to his trust, and your compatriot is not one possessed by *jinn;* for he saw him in the clear horizon.' The call-vision which was decisive for Mohammed was thus a vision which he saw out in the open. A being appeared to him whose majesty and glory so filled him with trembling awe as to assure him for all time that the voice which spoke to him did not come from a being of the *jinn* species. The heavenly messenger flew down, and when he had come very near he gave the future prophet a message, whose content was indeed kept reverently secret, but which probably constituted the direct commission to become Allah's prophet and messenger.

We may thus confidently affirm that the legend of the call which Ibn Sa'd accepted reproduces most faithfully the actual event. The vision in the cave is an earlier attempt to describe the call, in conformity with what was known of the experiences of poets and seers. Its chief motive is the repeated command of the angel to 'recite,' and it is based upon the belief that Sura 96 was the first revelation of the Prophet. But again, this is only an exegetical invention. How could the 'recital' of the Koran have begun, it was thought, if not with the command to recite: *Iqra*! Which was the first Sura was actually as little known to the earliest theologians of Islam as it is to us. There are many opinions, and several of them are much better substantiated than the opinion that it was Sura 96.

Was Mohammed's inspiration genuine? Did he speak in entire good faith? Formerly men thought that his character revealed a certain premeditation, a calculating cleverness, a preference for the sly methods of intrigue which could hardly be reconciled with an absolutely honourable character. Was he not dominated from the very beginning, when he first appeared as the Prophet of his people, by ambition and the greed for power?

That Mohammed acted in good faith can hardly be disputed by anyone who knows the psychology of inspiration. That the message which he proclaimed did not come from himself, from his own ideas and opinions, is not only a tenet of his faith, but also an experience whose reality he never questioned. Possibly he was in doubt at first as to the identity of the hidden voice—as to whether it really came from the heavenly messenger whom he had seen in the mountains of Mecca, or from an ordinary *jinni*. This latter possibility was so repugnant to him, not because there is an important external difference in the way in which a *jinni* and the way in which Gabriel delivers a revelation, but because he knew that his message had a different content and purpose than the babblings of a seer or the verses of a poet. It was a matter of eternal import, and not merely a petty concern of this world; it was in the sphere of things holy, not in that of things profane. The Christian conception, which identified the harmless and morally neutral *jinn* of popular belief with evil spirits, with devils or demons, was known in Arabia before Mohammed's day, and he soon adopted the same view. He also early accepted the Christian view that idol-worship is the work of the devil. For Mohammed the pagan gods are devils and *jinn* whom men have chosen to worship. But he also to some extent retains the ancient Arabian belief that the *jinn* are a kind of invisible counterpart to man. They are like men in being partly bad and partly good. According to Mohammed's own statement (Sura 72 and 46, 28) he recited the Koran to them in obedience to Allah's commands. Some of them were converted, and others persisted in their unbelief.

As I have tried to show in my work on *The Psychology of Mysticism*, there are two clearly differentiated types of inspiration: the auditory and the visual. In the former, revelation is a voice which speaks into the ear or heart of the prophet. The inner word which this inspired man passes on possesses, as a rule, a clear, concise, expressive, and frequently rhythmic form. Among literary artists we often find an obvious counterpart to this type of inspiration in the poets, especially in the lyric poets. 'One is not supposed to work but to listen. It is as if a stranger were speaking into your ears,' writes Alfred de Musset. But in the visual type of inspiration the message consists of visions and pictures, sometimes very clear and striking, but usually quite indefinite and deliquescent, and as fantastic as a dream. They further resemble dreams in that they occur in combination with a peculiar train of thought which accompanies the images like an explanatory text, telling us their meaning and their significance. In visual experiences this meaning often possesses a mysterious symbolic depth, which is divined rather than clearly grasped by the mind. The revelations which proceed from these images, and the meaning which the subject attributes to them, are sometimes characterized by a certain expansiveness and complexity that may often become quite tedious, and may take the form of prose narrative. Psychologically speaking, the lyrical inspiration is related to emotional excitement, to exaltation, whereas visual inspiration is related to the hypnotic states.

Mohammed apparently belonged to the auditory type. His revelations were dictated to him by a voice which he attributed to the angel Gabriel. An unintentional proof of the genuineness of his inspiration is given by Mohammed in Sura 75, 16, where we read: 'Move not thy tongue in haste to follow and master this revelation, for we will see to the collecting and recital of it; but when we have recited it, then follow thou the recital.' Many inspired persons have observed that any trace of intention, and any vestige of personal initiative, has a negative influence upon the free and spontaneous flow of inspiration. So the Prophet is not to move the tongue with the intention of forming in advance the words which the angel is about to speak. Calmly and quietly he is to wait for the recital of the angel, with the assurance that the divine words will remain ineradicably fixed in his memory (Sura 87, 8).

Inspiration, especially of the visual type, usually presupposes a certain psychic state, a more or less profound submergence or preoccupation of the mind. Sometimes this becomes complete unconsciousness. The earliest tradition[1] contains various details as to the external appearance and the process of revelation, some of which are without a doubt psychologically probable. 'Ayesha, Mohammed's favourite wife, relates: 'Once I witnessed how the revelation came to Allah's Apostle on a very cold day. When it was completed his brow dripped with perspiration.' According to another tradition Abdallah Ibn 'Umar asked the Prophet: 'Do you know when the revelation comes to you?' He replied: 'I

[1] Ibn Sa'd. i, 1, p. 131 f. Bukhari, *K. bad' al-wahi.*

hear loud noises, and then it seems as if I am struck by a blow. I never receive a revelation without the consciousness that my soul is being taken away from me.' Ibn Sa'd gives this saying of the Prophet: 'The revelation comes to me in two ways. Sometimes Gabriel visits me and tells it to me as though one man were speaking to another, but then what he speaks is lost to me. But sometimes it comes to me as with the noise of a bell, so that my heart is confused. But what is revealed to me in this way never leaves me.'

We often find in the tradition the statement that Gabriel came to Mohammed in visible form. It is even stated that the angel resembled a certain man, who is mentioned by name. This is part of the legend. Mohammed relates in Sura 53 that on two separate occasions he saw the being who gave him his revelations, and he describes the incidents in a way which clearly shows that the visions were strict exceptions. As is generally the case with inspired men receiving the auditory type of imagery, he seems to have had visions only at the beginning of his career. The midnight journey to Jerusalem, which his opponents in Mecca took more seriously than the Prophet himself desired, was probably a dream. Some authorities tell of his very intense sufferings and purely physical pains at the time of an inspiration. 'When the revelations came to the Prophet they pressed hard upon him, and his countenance darkened.' It even happened 'that he fell to the ground as if intoxicated,' and that he 'groaned like a camel's colt.' 'Ayesha, in a longer narrative, in which she plays the leading rôle, gives a noteworthy description, which is obviously both original and reliable: 'Then Allah's Apostle had his customary attack (the word here used is especially applied to attacks of fever, or rather to that stage of the attack in which the patient experiences intense heat), so that even though it was a very cold day, beads of perspiration rolled from his face.' On the basis of this statement it has long been thought that Mohammed was an epileptic. Even certain Byzantine writers made this discovery, and for a long time past Western writers have edified their readers with this compromising fact about the arch-enemy of Christianity. Even in recent times some authors have held fast to this idea, influenced by the scientifically superficial and hasty theory which the medical psychology of the past century made fashionable for a while, that the inspired state is 'pathological.' If, as is sometimes still argued, all types of semi-conscious and trance-like states, occasional loss of consciousness, and similar conditions, are all to be called epileptic attacks, then, of course, it can be said that Mohammed was an epileptic. But if epilepsy is to denote only those severe attacks which involve serious consequences for the physical and mental health, then the statement that Mohammed suffered from epilepsy must be emphatically rejected. Moreover, we can speak of his condition as being pathological only in the same sense in which inspiration is termed pathological in the case of many other religions, and in that of literary genius; that is, when it takes on striking and mentally abnormal forms. And too much credit should not be given to the traditional descriptions of the manner of the Prophet's revelations. Certain characteristics may be accurate, and they may agree with what we know concerning other inspired persons. The noises, the sound of bells, and the extreme heat are often mentioned by other inspired persons. But the whole atmosphere in the earliest congregation of Islam, its deadly earnestness and its strictness, will explain the fact that imagination likes to occupy itself with the supernatural 'gravity' of a revelation which forced the recipient to the ground. 'I saw,' according to one narrative, 'how the revelation came upon the Apostle of Allah as he was riding upon a camel. The animal groaned, and its legs slipped sideways, so that I expected it to collapse under the weight of the revelation. Soon it fell upon its knees, then tried to arise by planting its feet upon the ground.'[1] Obviously it is rash to draw psychological conclusions concerning the inspiration of the Prophet from the statements that have come down to us.

And it seems even more difficult to think of the lengthy

[1] Ibn Sa'd, i, 1, p. 132.

and often quite sober and prosaic decrees of the last years at Medina as the product of genuine and immediate inspiration. However, it is a natural enough process that an originally spontaneous inspiration should be transformed more and more into an inspiration of ideas, becoming increasingly subject to the control of the conscious will. We see how the Prophet gradually grew accustomed to think of ideas that emerged in his consciousness and decisions that matured in his soul as direct expressions of the Divine will. As far as I can see, such a development must be regarded as psychologically normal. In such circumstances we must beware of speaking of the conscious misuse or falsification of revelation.

But the genuineness of the revelation can and must also be interpreted in the deeper sense. Many a man whose inspiration has undoubtedly been psychologically genuine and direct has had nothing to give to his contemporaries. Such a man's consciousness of a call to prophecy apparently has no other basis than a pathologically exaggerated conception of the power and significance of his own personality. The content of his messages are more or less rational personal reflections, having no general interest or universal application. A genuine prophet is one who really has a message to deliver, one in whose soul some of the great questions of his age have stimulated a restlessness which compels him to speak, and for whom the ecstasy and prophetic inspiration are but the natural and inevitable expression of a strong lasting conviction and a genuine passion. Amos, the simple shepherd, comes to the national shrine at Bethel. He has no ready-made theory concerning his competence. Half confusedly he acknowledges: 'I am no prophet, neither am I a prophet's son. But Yahweh has spoken'—words conveying a sense of the majesty of law and righteousness which signify more than anything else in the world—'Who then should not prophesy?' —'The need which presses upon all classes of Christianity has forced me to cry out and speak,' writes Martin Luther.

Was Mohammed a genuine prophet? Had he truly a message to proclaim?

CHAPTER III

Mohammed's Religious Message

THE basic conviction of Mohammed's preaching, and the heart of his prophetic message, is the certainty that he alone, in the midst of a light-headed and thoughtless generation, sees the the fateful event which awaits all of those who are now jesting and laughing so carelessly. The threatening storm-cloud which already darkens the horizon, the disaster which seems so near that he regards himself as the 'naked messenger,' or the courier who arrives in tattered garments to give warning of the catastrophe which is already about to strike, is the *last day*—the day of judgment and retribution.

For him the Day of Judgment is not an occurrence far off in the hazy uncertain future, belonging to a different sphere from that of mundane events. It is a reality which is threateningly near. He speaks of it in the present tense. He seems to see how the heavens are being folded back above the heads of his careless countrymen, and how the black mountains of lava surrounding the city are collapsing like rubbish-heaps in terror before the advent of the Judge. Of course, Mohammed never stated directly that the judgment would fall upon his own generation, but rather that Allah alone knows when it will fall, and that no one, not even the Prophet, can say whether it is immediately impending. But, on the other hand, he often shows that he regarded it as possible that he himself might yet experience it.

His listeners misunderstood his use of the prophetic present tense. Days, months, and years passed, and the catastrophe did not arrive. They believed his prophecy to be false. 'When will the day really arrive which you have proclaimed?' his enemies scornfully inquired. To some extent the Prophet himself was to blame for this misunderstanding. For from the very beginning he spoke, in connection with his prophecy of the judgment, of actual punishments which God had inflicted upon godless cities and nations that refused to believe the warnings of the prophets. Like Christian preachers, Mohammed regarded these earthly punishments as precursors and preliminary steps to the final great judgment. And when he spoke of the flood, of thunderbolts, and of cyclones which came upon the generation of Noah and the generations of other prophets of old, he always concluded with a warning to his own nation: 'Thus shall the day of judgment come also upon this generation.' It was not until his last days in Mecca that the Prophet, now in utter despair over the unbelief of his countrymen, began definitely to suggest that Allah was preparing a special punishment for the rebellious cities, a punishment which would occur even before the day of judgment.

What the merchants of Mecca could not understand, and what certain learned Orientalists of our own day also find it hard to understand, is that Mohammed had no desire to be an apocalyptic seer, or a clairvoyant who foretells the exact time of the advent of the day of judgment. The present tense which he used expressed the unshakable certainty of his religious faith. The important thing for him is not *when* the day is coming, but the certainty that it *will* come. Man should so live, think, and act as though that day were already visible to the eye, being more certain of its reality than of anything else in this transient world.

In short and breathlessly stormy sentences, often with poetic rhythm and power, the earliest Suras of the Koran describe the great day of judgment, and the retribution which is sure to follow it. But the Prophet does not portray the events in a definite sequence as does a theologian who sets forth a dogmatic creed. He speaks as a messenger whose purpose is to awaken and to grip his listeners. In these scattered lines we see passing before us, as in a panorama, the tremendous imaginative religious experience which inspired the heart and conscience of Mohammed and made him a prophet.

A horrible natural catastrophe to which Mohammed gives various mysterious names—such as a thunderclap, a cry, a crash—will usher in the judgment. Either it will come simultaneously with a trumpet-sound which will call men before the Judge, or the trumpet-sound will produce it. The earth will be shaken by a terrific earthquake; it will be torn open, and will reveal what is hidden in its very depths. The mountains will be moved from their places; they will fuse together as in a mirage, will collapse into dust and ashes. The heavenly vault will totter and break, showing gaping fissures, or will be rolled up like a scroll. The edges of the disc of the sun will bend together, the moon will split apart and be darkened, the stars will be extinguished, and will fall in myriads to the ground. Thus Mohammed believed that the end of the world would be heralded by a tremendous earthquake. Further, the idea of a world conflagration is not absent from his thought. The heavens 'will give out a palpable Smoke' (44, 9) and a bright flash of fire, and molten brass will be hurled down upon men (55, 35).

At the first sound of the trumpet all living men, except a few of the very elect, will fall stunned to the ground. At the second sound of the trumpet all will arise, and the dead will emerge from their graves. The resurrection will occur in the twinkling of an eye. Quickly, 'as in a race,' the dead will leave their graves.

Behind the heavens, which have fallen down or have been rolled back, the throne of Allah will appear, borne by eight angels. The heavenly hosts will stand ranked in columns, and all men will gather before the throne. The good will be placed on the right, and the wicked on the left. Amid oppressive silence the trial will begin, and will be based upon the notes which are written in the Book of Deeds. Pious men will receive mild treatment, but sinners will be treated with the strictest justice. Their dark, dusty, and gloomy faces will speak against them, whereas the faces of the just will be radiant with joy because they are permitted to meet their Lord. No man can deny his sins. In addition to the words of the Book, the bodily members of the sinners, their hands, their feet, and their tongues, will testify against them. But

Allah will watch carefully to see that no soul receives unjust treatment. The prophets will be called forth, and they will testify that they proclaimed their messages of warning. Thus no man will be able to make the excuse that he was not warned. Sinners will seek in vain to place the blame upon the *jinn*—the devils who are supposed to have enticed them to idolatry. For the *jinn* will desert their former disciples, and will assert that these men have worshipped idols absolutely of their own free will. In their despair the unfortunate will seek help; but all in vain. In the judgment no soul can bear the burden of another; a father will not be able to do anything for his son, nor a brother for his brother. The doctrine of the mediation of the Prophet, according to which he will save each one of his disciples 'in whose heart there is only a speck of goodness,' is not confirmed by the Koran. There it is often stated that no mediation will be permitted and that none will avail on the day of judgment. There is only one hint that 'with Allah's permission' mediation may be possible, and in this case the angels are apparently thought of as the mediators.

After judgment has been passed will come the angels who are to execute punishment. They will seize the sinner, bind him with chains, and drag him away amidst scourgings and blows. They will be harsh and pitiless, relentlessly obeying Allah's strict commands. Under the command of the archangel, Malik, the guardian of hell, they will continue to torture the unfortunate ones in hell. They will force the victims to drink boiling water, crush their limbs with iron clubs, and clothe them in garments of fire. Although Mohammed does not spare himself in respect of the vividness with which he depicts the tortures of the damned, yet he does not even approach the frightfulness characterizing some of the Christian and Buddhist descriptions of the tortures of hell.

He takes much greater pains, on the other hand, in describing the joys of the redeemed in Paradise. Paradise is situated 'on high,' but whether this is in heaven, or on earth, like the Garden of Eden, is not clearly stated. It is a lovely place, filled with refreshing streams, where leafy bowers provide shade. The redeemed lounge upon divans and cushions, clothed in festive garments of silk and brocade. Gorgeous fruit-trees, pomegranates, bananas, grape-vines, and palms lower their fruit to those who wish to pluck it and furnish shade for those participating in the feast. They are also provided with meat of every kind, and with 'everything that they desire.' Youths as handsome as pearls walk about, serving a delicious drink which does not lead men into speaking foolishly or acting discreditably, nor does it cause headaches or dizziness. For entertainment and in marriage they receive the 'black-eyed Houris' of whom Mohammed states that they are virgins, chaste, and especially created by Allah. Although the Koran hardly provides a basis for such a view, the earliest tradition of Islam supports the definite conception that the virgins of Paradise were once earthly wives. The Prophet himself is supposed to have said: 'They are devout wives, and those who with grey hair and watery eyes died in old age. After death Allah re-makes them into virgins.'[1] That the wives and children of believers share in the joys of Paradise is self-evident for Mohammed, and is especially mentioned in several places.

In regard to the spiritual joys of Paradise Mohammed is more reserved. But we do discover that the redeemed rejoice because they need listen no longer to foolish talk, but may listen to the heavenly salutations of peace. They are no longer reminded of their sins (56, 24), but they praise Allah because He has taken away their sorrow (35, 31-32). And better than all else is Allah's good will and grace (9, 73).

A peculiar characteristic of Mohammed's conception of the future life should be especially stressed. The redeemed in heaven and the damned who are being tortured in hell are never called spirits or souls. He knows, of course, that man has a soul which is required of him at death, but for him a soul is not an existence without a body which is able to think, feel, and act. Mohammed probably conceived of the soul as

[1] Tabari, Tafsir xxvii, p. 96.

an impersonal power, a life-breath. When Allah takes the soul at death the man enters into a state of complete unconsciousness, as in deep and dreamless sleep. Where the souls are when Allah has taken them, whether they are really exterminated, or whether they survive in a dormant condition—these are questions which Mohammed does not discuss. At any rate, man does not again receive life and consciousness until the time of his resurrection. So the resurrection is actually a new act of creation. If the unbelievers scornfully inquire: 'How is it possible to receive life again after one has turned into decayed bones?' Mohammed replies by referring to the wonderful beginning of man in his mother's womb. He who first created man in his mother's womb out of a drop of running blood is surely able to awaken him—that is, to create him anew in the dark womb of the earth, and to bring him back alive.

But since the state between death and the judgment is a dreamless sleep without consciousness, it will seem to man that the judgment follows immediately upon death. This idea, which apparently impressed him very deeply, Mohammed expresses numberless times in the Koran. When man awakens at the resurrection he is asked his opinion as to how much time has passed since he died. The righteous ones, who know the truth because of their belief in the Koran, know that the day of resurrection has come, but the sinners are utterly confused. They swear that only an hour has passed, or that they have been in their graves for only a part of a day, or for a few days (10, 46 ff.; 46, 34 f., etc.). It is easy to see what an effect this theme of the Prophet's revival-preaching had. The hour of judgment, which seems so immeasurably distant to the unbelievers, will reach them before they are aware of it. There are no interminable intervals of time which must be passed. In the very same hour in which they have closed their eyes in death the reckoning is already at hand.

Another peculiarity of Koranic eschatology is partially explained by this conception. A number of passages of the Koran (75, 26 ff.; 56, 82 ff.; 6, 93 ff.) describe how angels will come and seize the soul at the critical hour of the death-struggle and will bring it before the Judge. Then they will take it immediately into fiery punishment. Obviously Mohammed is not thinking of a preparatory punishment before the final resurrection. For him the moment of death and judgment have become fused into a single event.

Mohammed makes one exception to the fate which must overtake all men, even believers: namely, the believing martyrs who have fallen in Allah's holy war. 'And repute not those slain on Allah's path to be dead. Nay, alive with their Lord are they richly sustained; rejoicing in what Allah of His bounty hath vouchsafed them, filled with joy for those who follow after them, but have not yet overtaken them' (Sura 3, 163-4). This belief that the souls of martyrs really exist, and enjoy the blessedness of Paradise before all others, is a Christian conception adopted by Mohammed, without his realizing that it is entirely incompatible with his idea of the soul and of its state after death.

What is there in this idea of judgment and retribution which so impressed Mohammed that he made it the pivotal point of his preaching? It is hardly because this belief is, in itself, convincing or probable. Within the soul of every man, even though he be a savage, there dwells a sceptic to whom the idea that a body which has decayed in the grave can become alive again is fantastic and unreasonable. It is too contrary to ordinary tangible experience. And Mohammed also met with stubborn unbelief at this very point. His countrymen rejected his preaching of the judgment and the resurrection as 'ancient fables.' Belief in the resurrection cannot find a support, as does the animistic belief in spirits and ghosts, in the unusual psychic experiences which to naïve thought constitutes a valid proof of the survival of the soul. This belief is paradoxical; it is rooted in a compulsion, an imperative of a different type from that of the logic of ordinary reason.

What made the Prophet certain that the message of the judgment and retribution must needs be true was a genuine glowing *faith in the God of judgment*, in His incomparable majesty, and His unqualified right to punish those who oppose His sovereign will. The real theme of Mohammed's preaching is rooted in religious experience, in a great and unique personal piety.

When Mohammed attempts to state the content of his faith in the briefest possible form he refers to it as 'belief in Allah and the last day.' The future life, with its judgment, underlies all other themes, like the deep bass of an organ; the belief in eternity determines the mood, and it is a mood of profound and ascetic earnestness. A believer should not only believe in the last day, but he should *fear* it—fear the judgment and the Lord of judgment. 'They who fulfilled their vows, and feared the day whose woes will spread far and wide' (76, 7). 'Believers are they who tremble in fear before the Lord.' When they call upon Allah their hearts tremble; when the Koran is recited the very skins of those who fear creep at it, and they fall upon their faces, weeping (39, 24; 17, 109). Even the most pious should fear. Not even the Prophet knows whether he and his followers shall escape God's punishment (67, 28). Fear, therefore, is no accidental mood which grips a man temporarily when he thinks of his sins and of Allah's strict justice, nor is it a mood which he may try to banish by holding up before his soul the comforting assurance of faith. Fear is the natural basic mood of piety; the pious man *should* be afraid.

For this reason the antithesis to the pious attitude is that of *levity and carelessness*. The godless indulge in a thoughtless life of indulgence; they carry on foolish and superficial conversation; they jest and play. Their hearts are filled with jovial levity, and they do all that their desires dictate. One sin of which the Prophet especially accuses them is that of 'indifference,' negligence. They never think of the future life, and do not believe in the final judgment. Therefore they will be stricken in their unpreparedness and ignorance.

Mohammed condemns worldly mindedness and secularity much as pietistic Christians do. Earthly life is empty and vain. A believer should regard the mundane and the temporal as something which is only a brief loan, an allowance for the journey to the eternal world. 'Know ye that this world's life is only a sport, a pastime, and a show, and a cause of vainglory among you! And the multiplying of riches and children is like unto plants which spring up after rain. Their growth rejoiceth the misbeliever; then they wither away, and thou seest them all sere; then they become stubble' (57, 19).

But if we may thus say that there is a pessimistic note in Mohammed's conception of earthly life, this pessimism is fundamentally no more radical than that which we find in the pietistic wing of Protestantism. Earthly life may be only a sport and a pastime, of little value when compared with the eternal future life, but it is not intrinsically evil and corrupt. Mohammed does not share the conception of later antiquity, and of Indian thought, that the flesh is itself injurious and valueless. He never tires of insisting that children and cattle, sowing and reaping, are gifts of Allah which man may use for his benefit and enjoyment. Navigation, metal-work, and caravans are means which Allah Himself has given for the support and well-being of man. But the eternal must not be crowded out by the temporal. 'Whoso would choose the harvest-field of life to come, to him will we give increase in this his harvest-field; and whoso chooseth the harvest-field of this life, thereof will we give him, but no portion shall there be for him in the life to come' (42, 19). These gifts easily become a temptation to man. It will profit him nothing to acquire great earthly goods. 'Should Allah bestow abundance upon His servants they might act wantonly on the earth; but He sendeth down what He will by measure' (42, 26).

The absolute earnestness which is always conscious of judgment and eternity lends a characteristic stamp to Mohammed's belief in God. His God is above all the strict righteous judge, before whose gaze the mountains collapse into dust and men stand in silence with bowed heads. God is the powerful, the almighty, the sublime. 'All that is in the heavens and in the earth praiseth Allah, and He is the mighty, the wise. His the Kingdom of the heavens and of the earth; He maketh alive and killeth; and He hath power over all things! He is the first and the last; the seen and the hidden' (57, 1-3). In His power and wisdom He accomplished the great work of creation, and He sustains it without effort. If He so desired He could annihilate the whole of humanity in a moment and raise up a new race in its stead. He sends punishments at will, and when He so desires He shows mercy and postpones His judgment. There are no laws or principles which restrain His will. It may be said, of course, that He is good, gracious, merciful, and righteous. But goodness and righteousness are not norms by which His conduct may be determined and predicted. Neither the Prophet nor anyone else knows what Allah's decision will ultimately be, and the prophecies and punishments of the Koran are expressly qualified in countless passages: So Allah wills!

The most remarkable implication of the Prophet's belief in Allah as sovereign, free, and indeterminable will is his doctrine of election by grace. Ultimately man's belief or unbelief does not depend upon his own desire and choice. It is Allah who grants or withholds the gift of faith, who either makes the heart receptive to warnings and revivals, or hardens the senses and veils the eyes of the soul.

The doctrine of predestination or divine foreordination seems to ordinary reason highly contradictory. It seems as though the certainty that God by an unchangeable decree has destined us in advance either to bliss or to damnation would cripple all desire and power of initiative, and would deprive men of any inclination to struggle on in the way of salvation, or would at least cripple all enthusiasm for the religious training of men, or for the preaching of reform and conversion. But as a matter of fact belief in foreordination has really the opposite effect. For it gives the human will new energy, and makes all earthly obstacles seem negligible and unimportant, and this gives man the courage to hope and to dare what is apparently impossible.

The explanation of this apparent contradiction is that belief in predestination is in fact the most profound and consistent expression of a purely religious conception of the world and of human life. The great and only significant and decisive thing which matters is God's majesty, His honour, His almighty, unconditioned will. This will, the cause and principle of all existence, cannot be forced, broken, or influenced by the rebelliousness and opposition of man. Man is not able to rebel against God's will and spoil His plan of salvation. The titanic rebellion of the godless man is a pathetic act of self-deception. He is only succeeding in doing what God has eternally decreed. At the same time (a contrast which unbelievers have difficulty in comprehending) the believer is assured, by the mercy which he has received through no virtue of his own, and contrary to his expectations, that this unfathomable will is in its very essence goodness and mercy; or, more precisely stated, it is the only norm of that which may be called goodness and mercy in this world. Many of the greatest geniuses of faith—St. Paul, Luther, and Calvin—have had similar ideas. It is a significant proof of the purely religious strength of Mohammed's experience of God that he arrived at this daring conception of the unbounded majesty and omnipotence of God without being influenced, as far as I can see, either by Judaism or by Christianity.

For Mohammed this belief seems to be taken for granted, even in conjunction with the first elementary conception of God as the king of the final judgment. One of the earliest Suras speaks of Him 'who has created the soul and given its wantonness and belief.' But apparently the unbelief of his countrymen, which, with his naïve and glowing faith in the truth and importance of his message, was to the Prophet, both a disappointing as well as an expected and incomprehensible thing, seems to have confirmed all the more his belief in Allah's unfathomable foreordination. The conviction which comforted and upheld him in the bitter years of struggle was the certainty that it was neither a defect nor impotency of the divine message, nor the weakness and disloyalty of him who had been commissioned to proclaim it, that caused the unbelief of his countrymen. Allah did not will their belief. 'But if thy Lord had pleased, verily all who are on earth would have believed together. What! wilt thou compel men to become believers? No soul can believe but by the permission of Allah, and He shall lay His wrath on those who will not understand' (10, 99-100). Even though the tangible miracles necessary to induce the heathen to believe were to happen, it would still be impossible for them to be converted unless Allah willed it. 'If there were a Koran by which the mountains could be set in motion, or the earth cleft,' and 'though we had sent down the angels to them, and the dead had spoken to them—they had not believed, unless Allah willed it!' (13, 30; 6, 111). And the Prophet even states expressly that Allah has purposely hardened the hearts of the unbelievers, so that it is impossible for them to believe. The unbelievers seek to refute the Koran, and make it an object of derision. 'Truly we have thrown veils over their hearts lest they should understand this Koran, and into their ears a heaviness; and if thou bid them to the guidance, yet even then they will never be guided (15, 55-56). Allah once made a vow to fill hell with men and *jinn*, and He intends to keep that vow. 'Had we pleased, we had certainly given to every soul its guidance. But true shall be the word which hath gone forth from me —I will surely fill hell with *jinn* and men together' (32, 13).

But it is not only in the unbelief of the wicked that Mohammed sees the irresistible power of God's will. It must also become apparent to believers that it is nothing but God's inscrutable will which works the miracles of grace in their souls. In Paradise the redeemed humbly acknowledge: 'We had not been guided had not Allah guided us' (7, 41). 'Yet as to him who shall be converted and believe and do the thing that is right, it may come to pass that he will be among the happy. And the Lord created what

He will and hath a free choice. But they have no power to choose' (28, 67-68).

Just as little as other religious leaders who have been forced, by the logic of a faith which offends reason, to believe in an eternal foreordination, was Mohammed conscious of the objection that predestination violates the free will of man and cancels his responsibility. When the Prophet looks at the matter from the human point of view he holds that it depends entirely upon one's own decision whether he shall choose belief or unbelief. For Allah is absolutely fair to man, and on the day of judgment He will conduct a formal trial to show the absolute justice of His action. The prophets will be called upon to testify that they have delivered the message of warning which was entrusted to them. The sinners will be unable to utter one word of self-vindication. Allah has done everything that can be expected of Him in sending a messenger with the clearly stated guidance to every nation. Man has only himself to blame, for 'the weighing on that day (is) with justice' (7, 7). In this connection Mohammed explains that the sinners themselves have, by their unbelief, lost the privilege of gracious guidance by which Allah leads men to faith, quite unconscious that there is any contradiction in this explanation (8, 23; 40, 10).

Along with this fundamental religious conception of Mohammed's—that is to say, his faith in Allah as unrestricted, inscrutable will—there is involved also another aspect of his god-concept which has usually been very harshly judged by Western criticism. Mohammed does not attribute unchangeableness to the Divine being. It is not enough that Allah's decision can never be changed by any outside power, but His will possesses in itself neither limits nor obstacles, which means that He never binds himself to a decision which He has once made. It is one of the mysteries of this unrestricted Divine will that Allah obviously cares nothing about being consistent. The Christian, and also the Jewish polemic of Mohammed's day, was extremely short-sighted when it assumed that it was merely a proof of the unblushing opportunism of the Prophet that he did not hesitate, when circumstances required, to change and rescind his earlier revelations, even when they contained specific commandments and instructions to the believers. It is true, of course, that this peculiarity of the Mohammedan doctrine of revelation is not unconnected with the character and personal make-up of the Prophet. But the ability to cling stubbornly and wilfully to a decision that has once been made, or to a previous opinion, even when it contradicts all reason, is not a sign of a superior spiritual personality. There are many absolute fanatics among religiously inspired persons who cling with an iron consistency to the most unfortunate and senseless ideas. But Mohammed was no fanatic. To a great extent the secret of his unique ability to attract men is explained by a wise yielding which was never deterred by principles. He had the courage to surrender a position which could not be held honourably. In Mohammed's case such wisdom, which characterizes all truly significant leaders and organizers, came into special conflict with his claim to be the transmitter of a Divine message which was inscribed upon the tablets safely preserved in heaven; a message, therefore, which ought to bear the stamp of the eternal and unchangeable. But in this conflict a healthy sense of realism conquered any fixity of principles. When circumstances required, Mohammed did not hesitate to assert that Allah had rescinded His former revelation and had substituted another. This principle is made clear in Sura 2, 100, which dates from the early period in Medina: 'Whatever verses we cancel or cause thee to forget, we bring a better or its like. *Knowest thou not that God hath power over all things?*' But apparently Mohammed had already used this method of changing earlier revelations, or of giving them a new content by means of explanatory or restrictive additions (compare 16, 103). We have already seen how in Sura 53 he kept on revising his utterances concerning the Meccan goddesses as his views changed in the direction of a stricter monotheism.

Two considerations should not be forgotten at this point,

if we would be fair to Mohammed. Firstly, and above all, he was not a man of letters. He had no definite idea of the unalterability of the written word. For him the written word was not a dead letter, but the eloquent living expression of a personal will. Secondly, the will which speaks in the Koran is unfathomable and incalculable. It is entirely consistent with Mohammed's conception of God that Allah cannot be held to a word which He has once spoken. If He so desires, He is free to change what He has previously decreed. Indeed, if He wanted to do so, He could even cancel the whole revelation which He has given to Mohammed (17, 88). No one can call Him to account for His actions. Another peculiar aspect of the irrational nature of the Divine will is that Allah often makes offensive or misleading statements in order to 'prove' men, or even to stir up unbelievers to contradict the revealed word (74, 31; 17, 43). Mohammed rightly feels that those who are lacking in an understanding of the religious content of his message are perplexed by what he thinks belongs only to the poetic and rhetorical trappings of the revelation. So Allah does not hesitate to give these smallminded and stupid souls special occasion for offence, in order to uncover the thoughts of their hearts.

Humble submission to Allah's Divine will is the inner essence of piety. However, it is quite wrong to think here only of the servile submission of the will. To be sure, everyone in heaven and on earth must submit, willingly or unwillingly, to Allah (3, 77). But religion is primarily a *voluntary surrender in trust and faith*. To designate this voluntary self-surrender of a believer to the Divine will Mohammed coined the term '*Islam*.' The Prophet himself was commanded to be the first of those who had submitted (*Muslim*) themselves: that is, the first of his own people, for the men of God and the believers of other nations also belonged to the submitters. As far as we know Mohammed himself coined the term which so fittingly expresses the basic characteristic of his piety. And he quite correctly used it also to designate the religion which he founded. 'The true religion with Allah is *Islam*: and they to whom the Scriptures had been given (Jew and Christians) differed not until after the knowledge had come to them, and through mutual jealousy. . . . If they shall dispute with thee, then say: I have surrendered myself to Allah as have they who follow me' (3, 17-18). The task, therefore, which is set before man in the face of the Divine will signifies not only the submission of the heart and will, but the absolute submission of the reason also to revelation. To propound and demand rational reasons for that which Allah has proclaimed and commanded is to 'dispute' about the Word. This is a presumption which has become fateful for the nations possessing sacred scriptures, and has caused them to split up into many sects which mutually combat one another.

However, the picture of the stern King of the Day of Judgment, the Almighty God to whose inscrutable will man can only submit, is made clearer by other traits. The God of Mohammed is also a gracious, a merciful, and a forgiving God. Unfriendly Christian critics often portray Mohammed's conception of the mercy of God as being pure caprice. In Christianity the love of God is called irrational, but in Islam capricious. Of course there is a difference between Christianity and Islam, and a very significant one. The thought that God has revealed His nature once and for all time as righteous and saving love is alien to Islam. And yet Mohammed himself undoubtedly had a certainty of God's grace and goodness. This certainty is related, primarily, to religious experience. Mohammed was conscious that since his earliest youth he had been an object of Allah's special care and protection, and that he was especially *called*. Allah found him fatherless and poor and gave him a home and riches (93). But superior to all earthly gifts are the riches of the spirit, the guidance and the Divine commission which the Prophet received through undeserved grace. Allah found him erring on the paths of paganism and brought him to the true faith (93, 7). He discovered that the Prophet's heart was filled with fear and unrest, and that his soul was depressed. Such unrest and fear are a sign of a secret hope which is so daring that it does not venture to stand boldly before the eyes of the soul, and which therefore appears in the guise of fear and perplexity. Hence they are, for the religious and the irreligious man alike, the precursors of a higher call and inspiration. Allah lifted this burden from and eased the heart of the Prophet. He exalted his name (94, 1-6), uniting it with His own when Mohammed, the son of Abdallah, become 'Allah's Apostle.' Mohammed undoubtedly spoke the real truth when he stated that he had never dared to dream that such an honour would come to him. 'Thou didst never expect that the Book would be given thee. Of thy Lord's mercy only hath it been sent down' (28, 86). And although he did confidently expect and hope that Allah would give the Arabs a sacred scripture which they could use for reading and prayers, yet he never once dared to admit even to himself that he hoped to be this new prophet. Consequently, the revelation was for him an absolute miracle, an unexpected and inexplicable act of Allah's mercy. That is the fixed point to which he refers again and again when the foundations of his faith waver. It is the truth which he *cannot* question, because it bears the marks of the reality of experience. In my opinion this unshakable faith in the miracle of revelation cannot be psychologically understood unless we can assume that it came to the Prophet himself as something entirely unexpected and unsurmised. With complete honesty he can assure us that his Koran was in no wise composed or constructed. And it is for this reason that the revelation and the prophetic call became the point at which Allah's inscrutable will appeared as an unexpected and undeserved act of grace. From that hour Mohammed regarded himself as the recipient of Allah's special providence and selection. He was under Allah's faithful care during the years of struggle in Mecca. Later he saw and understood that Allah had to spare the faithless city for his sake as long as he remained there. And he finally left his birthplace, and with a solitary companion fled to Medina. When they were forced to hide in a cave from his persecutors, Mohammed was able to comfort his frightened companion—according to tradition it was Abu Bekr, who later became Caliph—with the blessed assurance that Allah was surely with them. 'And Allah sent down His tranquillity upon him, and strengthened him with hosts ye saw not' (9, 40). The struggling young congregation in Medina was under the same wonderful guidance and protection. Hosts of angels fought at the side of the believers at Bedr. For Mohammed the victory was a definite proof that Allah was really on his side and supported his cause. In these events he saw the will of Allah historically revealed.

We are in the habit of pointing out that it is a religio-historical peculiarity of the prophets of Israel that they believed the God whom they proclaimed was a God of history. The gods of the tribal and nature religions have a more restricted sphere of action. To be sure, such deities also take a hand in the events of life. In a difficult situation they aid the individual as well as the nation. Odin grants victory to the heroes of Nordic legend, and the Olympian gods direct the Trojan War. And yet the religious interpretation of history of the Israelites is obviously of a quite different nature. Here we are dealing not merely with an occasional interference with the course of events, but God here makes Himself and His will known in the historical process. The prophets believed that Yahweh ruled and directed the historical process with unrestricted power, whereas in Nordic and also in Greek paganism the will of the gods was only one of the factors influencing events. Above them were the dark powers of fate, and in the last analysis these controlled the will of the gods and of men. Now Mohammed has the same point of view as the prophets of Israel; that is, that Allah alone rules over all. He believed in Allah's protection, and his conviction that he was the object of God's special care and guidance bears witness to a deep and genuine piety. We can acknowledge this without being blind to the fact that in thinking of predestination he did not always succeed in keeping himself entirely free from an element of selfishness and arrogance, although he feels this to be quite offensive in the case of the Jews, and sternly reprimands them for considering themselves to be the race favoured of God.

Of course Mohammed cannot ascribe any *motive* to Allah's goodness and grace. Its ultimate explanation is to be found in His inscrutable will. But it does not follow that the Prophet regarded Divine mercy as pure caprice. A certain sense of justice and fairness belongs to the nature of Allah. He has a just consideration for the weakness of man, and for the many uncertainties of life. The fact that Allah is fairly indulgent toward human frailty in its various forms is to the Prophet a sign of His mercy. It is significant that most of the additions which temper previous rules and commandments, especially those of the Medina period, have the purpose of relaxing the ordinances which were found to be difficult or impossible of fulfilment. If Allah has commanded devotional exercises, alms, and other tasks that become too great a burden for the growing congregation—which naturally cannot consist merely of perfect types—then He has pity upon believers and lightens the burden, 'for Allah is forgiving, merciful' (compare Sura 73, 20). And, therefore, since Allah proves to be just as free from formalism and fanatical obstinacy as the Prophet himself, it follows that Mohammed's personal character has influenced his conception of God in another respect also. Allah's mercy is especially evident in His acting generously and forgiving unbelievers their previous sins whenever they repent of their evil ways and do the works of faith (7, 151-152). He is no harsh unyielding avenger who insists upon absolute expiation for every atom of past guilt. This reminds us of the fact that Mohammed himself actually possessed a generous nature, that he was able to let the past be forgotten, and that he often showed an understanding of how to win over former enemies by magnanimity.

Mohammed's conception of *morality* is characterized by a peculiar tension between a purely religiously oriented ethic and a crass morality of reward and merit. When the religious view dominates man cannot depend upon his own merit, as if Allah were compelled to grant him the reward of Paradise for his good works. These good works are only a gift which Allah bestows upon the elect. The prayer of Augustine: 'Lord, give what Thou requirest, and require what Thou desirest' is appropriated also by pious Muslims: 'O Lord! stir me up to be grateful for Thy favours wherewith Thou hast favoured me and my parents, and to do good works which shall please Thee' (46, 14). To Mohammed the religious motive for a type of conduct that is pleasing to Allah is primarily *gratitude*. The Prophet's sense of God's transcendence is so strong that he speaks but rarely of love toward God (76, 8; 3, 29). On the other hand, the duty of being grateful to God is a theme which he never tires of elaborating. He constantly returns to the benevolence which Allah bestows upon man. He marvellously created him in his mother's womb, He sends rain from heaven and gives life to the dead earth so that it may sustain grass and seed; He has enriched man with cattle and has taught him metal-working, navigation, and commerce. And Allah expects man to be thankful for everything that He has given to him, and to show his gratitude by believing and by passing on some of these gifts to the poor.

On the other hand, when the practical application of moral demands is at stake, the Prophet cannot dispense with conceptions of reward and merit. Without considering Allah's foreordination, hell is portrayed as a punishment for the wicked and Paradise as a reward of the righteous. 'But for the God-fearing is a blissful abode, enclosed gardens and vineyards; and damsels with swelling breasts, their peers in age, and a full cup. There shall they hear no vain discourse nor any falsehood. A recompense from thy Lord—sufficing gift!' (78, 31-36). Especially when he is trying to inspire the believers to fight in the holy war for expansion of Islam, the Prophet resorts to the crassest formulations of the idea of rewards, in order to overcome their objections. 'Verily, of the faithful hath Allah bought their persons and their substance, on condition of Paradise for them in return. On the path of Allah shall they fight, and slay and be slain. . . . Nor give they alms either small or great, nor traverse they a torrent, but it is thus reckoned to them; that Allah may reward them with better than they have wrought' (9, 112, 122). A peculiar expression of what we regard as a crudely self-interested conception of moral conduct, is that good works are frequently called 'profitable business,' a good bargain. Whoever believes in Allah's book, prays and gives alms, makes a profitable bargain. To believe in Allah and His Apostle, and to fight against the enemies of Islam, is a bargain which results in deliverance from the torments of hell (35, 26; 61 10-11). Some think these commercial terms were a part of the professional jargon which Mohammed acquired as a business man and caravan traveller. We shall now attempt to show that they probably have another source.

We have already noted the appearance of a moral motive which may be said to be especially characteristic of Mohammed. That motive is the thought of the great and terrible Day of Judgment, which arouses man to moral earnestness and impels him to do good works. This obviously involves a tendency toward a morality of rewards. The fear of punishment and of retribution cannot be counted among the higher ethical motives. However, we should be doing Mohammed an injustice if we thought that this trembling before the Day of Judgment involved nothing more than fear of punishment. The 'fear of God' is more than being afraid. Trembling in awe before the King of the judgment day arouses a feeling of the tremendous seriousness of life, and of the responsibility and sublimity involved in being Man. The element of holiness enters the soul and bows the heart in willing obedience. So the fear of the Day of Judgment is quite naturally allied to the motives of gratitude and love toward God. Allah's servants 'fulfil their vows and fear the day whose woe will spread far and wide.' They 'bestow their food on the poor and the orphan and the captive,' saying: 'We feed you for the sake of Allah. We seek from you neither recompense nor thanks. A stern and calamitous day dread we from our Lord' (76, 7-10; compare 23, 62). Therefore this motive, which occupies a very prominent place in the moral preaching of the Koran, as well as in earlier Mohammedan piety in general, often possesses a deeply religious undertone. Of course this does not prevent the fear of judgment from often degenerating into a primitive fear of hell, and from being exploited even in the Koran, and still more so later on, in a way which makes the moral attitude of Islam seem external. Mohammed does not hesitate to frighten those stingy people who begrudge giving the prescribed alms. He assures them that the wealth which the unjust have acquired will be hung around their necks on the resurrection day. And he tells the believers: 'If ye do well, to your own advantage will ye do well, and if ye do evil, against yourselves will ye do it' (17, 7).

The morality which the Koran proclaims is apparently of a definitely social nature. The duty of being kind and helpful is especially stressed. The wealthy have the responsibility of aiding the poor with their surplus. Since Mohammed frequently insists that an occasional gift is not sufficient, that alms-giving must be regarded as a perpetual responsibility, a sort of permanent institution, and that the believer is to give the needy man 'a share' of his possessions, it is quite understandable that Hubert Grimme, in a book which attracted a great deal of attention in its day, championed the idea that Mohammed should be treated as a social rather than as a religious reformer. According to Grimme, the social injustices prevailing at the time in Mecca, where the wealthy merchants oppressed the poor and allowed them to perish in their misery, aroused the flaming wrath of the Prophet, and he arose to establish a new and better social order.

It is quite probable that in a city like Mecca, where the populace was dependent primarily upon commerce, poverty must have been intense in hard times, and it is more than probable that in accordance with ancient Arabian conceptions social responsibility did not extend beyond the members of one's own tribe (compare 36, 47). So there were certainly concrete reasons for Mohammed's espousal of the obligation of mercy. However, we must not form exaggerated conceptions of the social need in Mecca. The little town in the lava mountains was no Arabian Babylon, and the rich merchants were certainly not completely divorced in their habits and the circumstances of their life from the remaining populace. On the other hand, the standard of living was low. The Bedouin often had to experience hunger and privations, and the poorer elements in the city were certainly no better off. At all events, it is absolutely wrong to regard Mohammed's social interest as the primary factor. Expressions of sympathy with the poor are not lacking. Like all noble characters, Mohammed certainly felt a real and sincere concern for the poor and neglected. But we find in him no real indignation concerning their hard lot, and still less did it occur to him to attempt to abolish poverty. Pious gifts are not made for this purpose. Alms are given for Allah's sake because they are pleasing to Him, or they are given for one's own benefit, for the 'cleansing' of the soul, to eradicate the effects of sin committed, or to prevent accumulated wealth from becoming a damning burden on the Day of Judgment, or to store up good works with which to earn Paradise.

Mohammed's motive for benevolence is, then, quite different from the natural feeling of solidarity, the duty of helping one's tribesmen, which, among primitive peoples, usually acquires a religious character, being often a sacred custom, guarded by the chief deity. Still less is it based upon the Bedouin conception of the virtue of generosity. The pagan Arabs placed a high value upon charity. It is chivalrous trait. *Karim* means both noble and generous. Charity arouses admiration; indeed, when practised in the royal style it is praised as much as bravery and valour in battle. With a quick gesture, carelessly and royally, the noble man gives to the first man who asks. Without deliberation, and without stopping to think that he himself may be impoverished on the morrow, he butchers hundreds of camels and invites all who will to come to the feast. This impulsive and extravagant generosity, just for the mere joy of playing the royal benefactor for a brief moment, which is characteristic of individuals and groups for whom poverty is the normal condition, is praised in Arabic poetry and legend as a proof of genuine nobility. However, Mohammed was very critical of this Bedouin ideal. He rightly felt that such giving was by its very nature and purpose the direct opposite of that almsgiving which Allah loves. And pointing directly to this boastful and extravagant charity, he says in admonition: Give, 'yet waste not wastefully, for the wasteful are brethren of the Satans. . . . Let not thy hand be tied up to thy neck; nor yet open it with all openness, lest thou sit thee down in rebuke, in beggary' (17, 28-31).

It may seem quite natural that charity and helpfulness should be placed foremost in the list of virtues. Food, clothing, and other bodily necessities achieve a prominence, especially under primitive conditions of life, which cannot be overlooked. Only gradually does it become evident that man does not live by bread alone, but that with the more complex development of life other duties take equal rank with charity. Nor is the unique reason which Mohammed advances for almsgiving bound up with the savage ethic. On the contrary, it is typical of some highly developed religions. We meet with it in Parseeism, in later Judaism, and in Catholic Christianity. This whole attitude, which is characteristic of a certain type of benevolence, is always present whenever man's attitude to the next life becomes especially dominant. Its psychological basis is the feeling that the world beyond tends to lose its value and its reality the more we are completely satisfied with the present, and really feel at home in this world. When this world is small and miserable the soul can lift its wings to the eternal and unchanging world beyond. Therefore wealth, with its capacity for creating comfort and satisfaction in this world, is regarded as a sworn enemy of the religious sense of eternity. Logically the religious man should give up all his possessions, but naturally he seldom has the courage to be so consistent, and so almsgiving becomes a fitting substitute. Consequently it is not actually a social duty, but a ritual act, a gesture by means of which the religious man tells his God what his attitude really is. And like other symbolic acts it relieves the burdened conscience, and gives man the feeling that he is really accomplishing that which almsgiving symbolizes—namely, emancipation from possessions. Hence it is self-evident that for this type of piety God, the Eternal, as the highest personal value, is the recipient of such alms. The gift is offered to God, and the question of who is to receive it here on earth is ultimately of little importance. Such charity has nothing whatever to do with altruistic social interests. 'My fathers gathered that which bears no fruit. I have gathered that which bears fruit. My fathers gathered treasures of Mammon; I have gathered the treasure of the soul. My fathers gathered for others; I have gathered for myself. My fathers gathered for this world; I have gathered for the next.' Thus, according to the Talmud, King Monobazus of Adiabene prayed.[1] It is unadorned religious selfishness which so exaggerates pious benevolence.

However, we see a survival of genuine Arabian ethics when Mohammed so frequently mentions destitute relatives in speaking of the poor who should be remembered with alms. As recipients of pious charity the fatherless, wayfarers, and prisoners are likewise included. The freeing of a slave is regarded as an especially virtuous act, and is demanded as an act of penance from those who have unintentionally killed a believer.

[1] Bousset, *Die Religion des Judentums in spät-hellenistischen Zeitalter*, third ed., p. 141.

In Mohammed's time it was already customary that believers should bring their alms to the spiritual leader of the congregation; in other words, almsgiving was in process of being transformed into a type of taxation. According to Sura 9, 60, alms should be given to the poor and needy, and also to those who have the task of collecting it, and to those whose hearts are to be won to Islam—a type of bribery therefore, used to buy off political opponents—and finally, they are to be used to purchase the freedom of slaves, for debtors, and for poor wayfarers. In Medina the alms of the believers became a mighty politico-economic weapon in Mohammed's hands.

Among other moral duties Mohammed emphasizes reverence and gratitude toward one's parents: Show 'kindness to your parents . . . and say not to them, "Fie!" neither reproach them. And defer humbly to them out of tenderness; and say: Lord, have compassion on them both, even as they reared me when I was little' (17, 24-25). Mohammed commands men to be honest in business and conduct, loyal, true to their word, humble, and peace-loving: 'And the servants of the Merciful are they who walk upon the earth softly; and when the ignorant address them, they reply: Peace!' (25, 64).

Apart from the really liberal freedom which Mohammed's marriage regulations allow to the sexual instinct—a man may have four wives at the same time, and in addition he has jurisdiction over his slave women—the believer is to practise restraint and chastity. Women should be decent and should modestly lower their glances. They are to display their charms only to their husbands or very near relatives. This rule hardly involves the duty of wearing a veil, but this custom was later adopted from Persian and Syrian Christians. Men must treat their wives with kindness and friendliness. Although Mohammed advocated treating the weaker sex with justice and consideration, he was by no means in favour of the emancipation of women. The strict patriarchal system and the restriction of woman's freedom of movement which he attempted to enforce would seem to imply a retrogression as compared with the freedom frequently enjoyed by Arabian women. It can only be said in Mohammed's defence that he was trying to introduce into Islam the customs of more highly civilized neighbouring peoples. Moreover, the women of the masses, thanks to the independence which the value of their work gave them, never completely submitted to this anti-feminist legislation. Sura 4, 38 gives an idea of what a Mohammedan husband may expect of his good loyal wife: 'Men are superior to women on account of the qualities with which Allah hath endowed the one above the other, and on account of the outlay they make from their substance for them. Virtuous women are obedient, careful during the husband's absence, because Allah hath of them been careful. But chide those for whose refractoriness ye have cause to fear; remove them into beds apart, and scourge them; but if they are obedient to you, then seek not occasion against them.' If Mohammed's crass insistence that a wife's person is at the disposal of her husband is offensive to us, let us not forget that the ethics of the Lutheran Church, in the familiar catechism of Bishop Emporagius, likewise counts a wife as the property of the husband.

Mohammed was unable completely to abolish blood-vengeance. Apparently it was too deeply rooted in the legal conceptions of the Arabs. But he attempted to check the most striking abuse of this primitive custom by stipulating that only *one* life could be taken, the life of a free man for a free man, of a woman for a woman, of a slave for a slave. Unintentional homicide does not give one the right to blood-vengeance. The kinsmen of the victim must be satisfied with a settlement consisting of one hundred camels for a man and fifty camels for a woman.

Even in his early years Mohammed violently opposed the cruel custom of killing infant girls which prevailed in Arabia.

For the Mohammedan, services of worship and religious exercises are not primarily a gift, a privilege of being able to experience the joy and riches of the Divine presence. They are a duty, an obligation to Allah. That does not mean, of course, that the inspiration and peace of prayer are unknown to Mohammedan believers. Mohammed is supposed to have said of himself: 'Three things have been especially dear to me in this world. I have loved women and pleasant odours, but the solace of my heart has been prayer.' It is possible that the Prophet actually uttered this saying, with its naïve yet fitting self-characterization. At all events, it is true that Mohammed did not place such great importance upon any other religious duty as he did upon prayer. Even to-day the hour of prayer, called out from the gallery of the slender minaret by the Muezzin, the melancholy modulation of his voice reminding us of the old Gregorian chant, lends to the Mohammedan city its unique character, and for a long time —although recently the tidal wave of indifference has reached even the devout Orient—the readiness with which the call to prayer was heeded in the streets, markets, and bazaars attracted the humble admiration of Christian observers.

By prayer, *salat*, Mohammed does not mean quite the same as we do. He does not mean the conversation of the heart with God, the calling and asking for support and aid. Prayer in this precise sense is known also. In Arabic it is called *du'a*, calling. And a believer may insert such personal prayers at a definite place in the official ritual of prayer. The *salat* is more like our public worship. It consists of reading the scriptures—the worshipper reads or repeats from memory the first Sura of the Koran, 'Fatiha,' and other short Sura or verses—of reading or reciting the confession of faith, of the benediction or petition for the Prophet, and of brief praises, all of which must all be recited with minutely prescribed bowing, kneeling, and prostration. The believer is permitted to practise this worship wherever he may happen to be. In the city, to be sure, a group always gathers in the mosque, but the only religious obligation is participation in the prayers at the prayer service on Friday at noon. The choice of Friday as the day of common worship dates from the Prophet's period in Medina, and reveals, with touching naïveté, both the dependence of the Prophet upon Judaism and Christianity and his endeavour to be independent of the religions of the Bible. However, Mohammed's day of worship is not a day of rest. According to the prescription of the Koran (62, 9-10), only during the time of the noon prayer must the believers refrain from work. The present-day regulations concerning public prayer date from a later time. We know nothing certain about the form of the ritual during Mohammed's lifetime. However, the reading of the Koran apparently occupied the most prominent place, and bowing, kneeling, and prostration, the believer touching the ground with his forehead, were then, as now, part of the ritual. The daily seasons of prayer, which to-day number five, were originally only two. 'Observe prayer at sunset, till the first darkening of the night, and the daybreak reading—for the daybreak reading hath its witnesses, and watch unto dawn in the night; this shall be an excess in service' (17, 80-81). So Mohammed and his followers in Mecca observed only the evening and morning prayer. In Medina another prayer at three in the afternoon was added, evidently in imitation of the three periods of prayer of the Jewish congregation.

The night watch which was recommended as a voluntary religious exercise came to take an important place among religious duties. In Sura 73, 1-6 Allah admonishes the Prophet himself to observe such nocturnal vigils: 'O thou enfolded in thy mantle, stand up all night, except a small portion of it, for prayer; half; or curtail the half a little—or add to it. And with measured tone intone the Koran, for we shall devolve upon thee mighty words. Verily, at the oncoming of night are devout impressions strongest, and words are most distinct.' It is no light ascetic practice which is here demanded of the Prophet. The faithful must follow his example. Servants of mercy are 'they that pass the night in the worship of their Lord prostrate (at the songs of praise) and standing' (while reading the Koran) (25, 65), and it is said of the redeemed in Paradise: 'little of the night was it that they slept, and at dawn they prayed for pardon' (51, 17-18). In a noteworthy addition which Mohammed made to Sura 73 in Medina, Allah declares that He knows well that the Prophet and his followers watch somewhat less than 'two-thirds, or half, or a third of the night.' He knows that they do not count the hours exactly which they devote to these nightly devotions, and that there are some sick and infirm, and others who must work for a livelihood among them. Therefore each one is permitted to read as much of the Koran as he is able. So the vigils were kept in Medina also and some of the believers tried scrupulously to live up to the former strict teaching. But Mohammed possessed too much healthy practical sense to allow pious asceticism to be made an end in itself. By no means does he wish to abolish the vigils, but the long watches are impossible for the great majority of the congregation, and this demand must be adapted to circumstances. Like many of the Christian ascetics, Mohammed was compelled later on to retreat from his original all too strict requirements.

Much of the attitude which we have just described is familiar to us. The material for the spiritual structure erected by the Prophet of Islam evolved from the world of ideas which is common to Christianity and Judaism. When one examines each of the elements of Mohammed's system of belief, it seems impossible to decide to which of these religions he is most indebted. However, there is evidence that the Jewish element in the Koran becomes more prominent as the personal development of the Prophet progresses. The insight which he gradually acquired from the beliefs of peoples who possessed sacred scriptures came mostly, especially in Medina, from Jewish sources.

But it is otherwise with regard to the internal relations, the spirit which unites the various elements into a whole. Fundamentally the heart of Mohammedan piety is, of course, a personal creation based upon a religious experience which constitutes in itself a new chapter in the history of religion.

But that does not preclude the fact that in important respects this experience shows a close relationship to other movements in the history of religious experience.

The deep earnestness, the keen expectation of future life, the contrition and trembling before the Day of Judgment, fear as an actual proof of piety, the warning against the carelessness which forgets responsibility and retribution: these things form also the basic mood of *Christian ascetic piety* as it survived in the Oriental churches, and where likewise it had become the ideal and norm of the laity in a much higher degree than was the case in the West. Ammonas, the pupil of Pachomius, has impressively described the spirit in which the genuinely pious should live. The monk should always feel like the imprisoned criminal, who merely awaits the time when he shall be brought before his judge. He should continually ask himself: 'How shall I be able to stand before the judgment of Christ, and what shall I answer in his presence?'[1] As a theme for the meditation of the monk, Euagrius specifies the perishability of life, the day of death, and the condition of the damned in a terrible hell. 'Remember also the day of resurrection, when you shall stand before God. Think of that which awaits sinners, of confusion before God and His Christ, angels and archangels and powers, and all men; of the places of punishment, the eternal fire, the worm which dies not, of Tartarus, the darkness, the gnashing of teeth, the horror and fear.'[2] Fear of the last judgment does not belong merely to the preliminary stages of the path of faith; it is not something which the mature experience of faith must overcome. It is characteristic of all really genuine piety; the believer *must cultivate fear*. It is the only road to salvation. The more fear, the more tears and contrition, the higher the stage of perfection. Three monks came to Father Sisoes and complained that they were continually pursued by the fear of three things: fear of the river of fire, of the worm which dies not, and of the outer

[1] Migne, P. G., *Apophthegmata patrum*, lxv, p. 120.
[2] *Ibid.*, *Rerum Monach. rationes*, xl, p. 1262.

darkness. When the saint made no reply they were greatly depressed. Finally he said: 'My brothers, I envy you. As long as such thoughts live in your souls it will be impossible for you to commit a sin.'[1] It is often said that the famous monastic saints wept during their last hours because of their fear of the approaching day of reckoning—and legend took this to be a proof of the depth of their piety. Throughout his life Arsenius wept so much that he always had to keep a cloth on his lap as he worked, in order to catch his tears. As the hour of his death approached his disciples saw him weeping, and asked him: 'Do you also, father, cultivate fear?' He answered: 'The fear which I feel at this hour has been in my heart ever since I became a monk.' Thus he passed away.[2] Three days before his death Agatho lay motionless and his eyes open. His disciples asked: 'How do you feel?' He answered: 'I am standing before the judgment-seat of Christ.[3]

In contrast to this terror-stricken watchfulness the true nature of godlessness and worldliness is described as carelessness and neglect. The time which he spent out in the world the monk calls 'the time of my heedlessness.' Just as the Koran so often tells how the unbelievers foolishly jest and laugh, so the monastic fathers likewise warn believers against laughing and joking. Smiles and thoughtless chatter are like fire in dry reeds. 'Do not smile, my brother,' says Father Ammon, 'for if you do, you will drive the fear of God from your soul.[4]

And in the Syrian churches we discover the same world-negating piety, the same fear of judgment and eternity. The Syrian monks thought the ability to weep was proof of an exceptionally high degree of piety. According to legend, St. Thomas lived in a cave and wept day and night, continually repeating to himself: 'Life has passed, death comes, de-

[1] *Book of Paradise*, ed. Budge, i, p. 631.
[2] *Apoph, patr.*, p. 105.
[3] *Ibid*, p. 117.
[4] *Book of Paradise*, i, p. 632.

struction approaches, the hour of judgment has arrived.'[1] Of another saint it is told that he wept and howled like a jackal over his lost life, his sins, death's approach, and the terrible judgment of righteousness.[3]

In order to arouse and warn careless and confident men of the world the Syrian fathers admonish them to reflect upon the ultimate fate of all human glory. *Ubi sunt qui ante nos*! 'Think, my friends, and consider how many former generations were allowed to remain in this world. Death has removed the past generations, so strong, powerful, and wise,' writes Aphraates.[3] Likewise Mohammed admonishes his proud countrymen to learn a useful lesson from the message of transiency: 'Have they not journeyed in this land, and seen what hath been the end of those who flourished before them? More were they than these in number, and mightier in strength, and greater are the traces of their power remaining in the land, yet their labours availed them nothing' (40, 82). As a warning edifying stories are often told of how God's judgment has struck the hardhearted and unmerciful rich. Near the home of the holy Abraham there lived a powerful man who brought fear to the poor and sighs to widows and orphans. When the oppressed people complained of him to the holy man he was warned of the judgment of God, but he paid no attention to the words of warning. But one night his house caught fire and was burned to ashes, along with many treasures. He lost all his possessions; in two years all his vineyards and orchards were destroyed.[4] And Mohammed tells also of the 'owners of the garden' who swore that no poor man should share the harvest with them, and as a punishment the next morning they found their garden ruined by a storm (68, 17 ff.; 2, 268). And just as Mohammed never tires of describing how Allah's punishments—'thunderbolts,' or earthquakes, or hurricanes, struck the godless nations of old who would not heed the warnings of their prophets—so the Syrian preachers relate that after the flood similar

1 Land, *Anecdota syriaca*, ii, p. 90.
2 *Ibid*, ii, p. 108.
3 *Aphraates* (Bert), p. 355.
4 *Anecdota syriaca*, ii, p. 90.

punishments—earthquakes and hurricanes—descended upon the idolatrous nations, demolishing their proud dwellings. 'And in the days of Nahor, in his seventieth year, when God saw that men worshipped idols, there came a great earthquake. And they all fell backwards, all their buildings were overturned and collapsed. Yet they took no heed in their hearts, but only increased their wickedness the more.' . . . 'And in the hundredth year of Nahor, when God saw that men sacrificed their children to demons and worshipped idols, God opened the storehouse of the wind and the gate of the storm, and a blast of wind rushed over the whole land. It cast down the statues and altars of the demons, brake together the idols and the altars of sacrifice, and heaped upon them great hills which remain to this day. The teachers call this gale the whirlwind "*taupana de rucha*." '[1] Compare this with Sura 41, 15; 17, 70; 29, 39. With the phrase 'they . . . only increased their wickedness' compare 17, 84.

As in the Koran, so in Syria the eschatological motive, fear of the Day of Judgment and of the great reckoning, is the dominant motive for good works. Among the works of piety almsgiving is of greatest importance, and the poor in especial are mentioned as objects of religious charity, as well as prisoners and wayfarers. The last two groups are especially typical of the benevolence of the Oriental churches. From the obligation of caring for prisoners and persecuted fellow-believers, prison welfare work was developed. Hospitality to travelling brothers was a precious obligation for the Syrian monks, since they often wandered about and lodged with holy ascetics and hermits. Here, too, we find the origin of the commercial expressions which characterize Mohammed's religious vocabulary. Alms wipe out sins and bestow upon the giver 'a profitable reward in the next world.' Often almsgiving is described as a 'profitable business.' By means of good works the believer carries on a 'bargain of righteousness.'[2]

[1] Bezold, *Die Schatzhöle* (Syrisch and Deutsch), pp. 132, 134.

[2] Andrae, *Ursprung des Islams*, K.H.A., 1925, p. 88.

To an extent to which these brief references naturally cannot do justice, the similarity between Mohammed's religion and Syrian Christianity appears not only in the general agreement of the content of ideas, but also in expression, form, and style of preaching. In this connection a study of Afrem (Ephraim the Syrian), the greatest preacher of the Syrian church, is instructive. This church father, who was held in the highest esteem both by Monophysites and Nestorians, discussed no other subjects with such partiality and such rhetorical power as the eschatological themes: death, the judgment, and eternal rewards. We find many points of similarity between his sermons on the judgment and the well-known descriptions of the Koran, even the expressions and images being often in striking agreement. A glance at Afrem's *Hymns of Paradise* is of special interest. As a proof of the religious inferiority of the Arabian prophet, Christians have often pointed out that Mohammed depicts eternal bliss merely as an endless and unrestricted satisfaction of extremely primitive sensual desires. The polemical ardour should be damped by what seems to me to be the irrefutable fact that the Koran's descriptions of Paradise were inspired by the ideas of this Christian Syrian preacher. Afrem's *Hymns of Paradise* depict the joys of the blessed in very mundane colours. 'I saw the dwelling-places of the just, and they themselves, dripping with ointments, giving forth pleasant odours, wreathed in flowers and decked with fruits. . . . When they lie at the table the trees offer their shade in the clear air. Flowers grow beneath them and fruits above. Their roof is composed of fruits and their carpets are of flowers. . . . Swift winds stand before the blessed, ready to do their will. One of them wafts appeasement, another causes drinks to flow. One wind is filled with oil, another with ointment. Who among you has ever seen the winds act as servants! or breezes which one may eat and drink! In Paradise the winds give nourishment in a spiritual fashion to spiritual beings. It is a feast without effort, and the hands do not become tired. . . . Think, O aged one, of Paradise! When its aroma refreshes you and its pleasant odours renew your youth, your blemishes will vanish in the beauty which surrounds you. Let Moses be an example to you. His cheeks, which were covered with wrinkles, became beautiful and radiant. This is a mystical symbol, showing how age shall be rejuvenated in Paradise.' The wine which the redeemed enjoy is lifewise not lacking in the Christian Paradise, and one may recognize a veiled reference to the virgins of Paradise in Afrem's saying: 'Whoever has abstained from wine on earth, for him do the vines of Paradise yearn. Each one of them holds out to him a bunch of grapes. And if a man has lived in chastity, they (feminine) receive him in a pure bosom, because he as a monk did not fall into the bosom and bed of earthly love.'[1] To be sure, Afrem occasionally points out that this is only an attempt to give some idea of a joy which no earthly mind is able to grasp. But most of his listeners and readers no doubt remained quite oblivious to his feeble attempts to spiritualize his sensual images. Popular piety certainly interpreted this daring imagery in a crass and literal sense, and under such circumstances one cannot blame a citizen of pagan Mecca for doing the same thing.

Mohammed's devotional exercises also strongly remind us of those which were performed by the Syrian monks and hermits, and even for a shorter or longer period by Christian laymen, as expressions of their religious awakening or their intense piety. Nightly vigils of prayer and recitation, particularly of the psalms, occupy the first place among the spiritual exercises of the monks. When Mohammed prescribes for himself and his followers that they shall watch half the night and recite the Koran, he is repeating the classical rules for the vigils of the monks. Pachomius commanded his dis-

[1] *Ap. syr.*, iii, pp. 563 ff.

ciples to watch through half of the night.[1] Macarius lays down the same rule, primarily as a precaution against an exaggerated ascetic fervour: 'Half the night will be sufficient for your devotions. The other half is for the rest of your body.'[2] This noctural worship consisted of a period of reciting the sacred scriptures, alternating with a period of chanting and prayerful sighing of equal length. Definite bodily postures were observed: standing, kneeling, and prostrating oneself so that the forehead touched the ground. As proof of a holy man's piety it is often reported that his forehead showed definite marks of his continual prostrations.[3] And Mohammed also states that his true followers have marks on their faces from their continual prostrations (48, 29). The Mohammedans and the Syrian Christians both counted the length of their devotions by the number of kneelings.

The characteristics which have been described so far are common to the Oriental churches in general. But in my opinion an especially important conception, which is peculiar to the Koran, makes it possible for us to decide more definitely where Mohammed got his most important suggestions. I refer to Mohammed's doctrine that the soul sinks into complete unconsciousness after death, so that the Day of Judgment seems to follow immediately after death. At that time such an idea existed only in the *Nestorian Church* in Persia. Previously the Syrian church father Aphraates taught that the soul exists in a state of deep sleep between death and the judgment,[4] but about 580, that is, about thirty years before Mohammed appeared as a prophet, Babai the Great, one of the most prominent theologians of the Nestorian Church, had again advanced the theory that the soul could not function without the body. Man is a corporeal entity, en-

[1] *Vie de Pachome*, Annales du Musée Guimet, xvii, p. 347.
[2] *Vertus de St. Macaire*, *ibid.*, xxv, p. 167.
[3] John of Ephesus, *Patr. Orient.*, xvii, p. 40. An Arabian poet describes a monk who had a bump on his forehead like the knee of a goat, from his many prostrations. Cheikho, *an-Nasraniyyu*, p. 178.
[4] *Aphraates* (Bert), p. 141.

dowed with reason. Considered by itself, the soul is not a complete entity. To be sure, the soul may be said to continue its existence as a substance after the dissolution of the body, but it lacks knowledge and memory. Besides quoting scriptural passages to prove this theory, Babai also cites the legend of the seven sleepers,[1] which Mohammed likewise used for the same purpose (18, 8-24). This teaching was apparently not a heretical innovation, but merely expressed an idea which was general in the Nestorian Church. For a long time Babai was himself the actual leader of the Church, and finally its highest office was offered to him. This doctrine dominated the Nestorian Church for centuries. As late as the tenth century it was ordered that those who believed that the soul possesses consciousness after death should be excommunicated. In my opinion this, along with other reasons, proves that Mohammed received from the Nestorians of Persia the impressions which decisively influenced his personal religious message. The Christian Arabs in Hira, on the border of Mesopotamia, with whom the Meccans were in especially vital contact, belonged to the Nestorian Church.

However, this by no means solves the riddle of Mohammed's relation to Christianity. Although he betrays his relationship to Oriental Christianity in certain important respects (which cannot possibly have been accidental), in other respects he shows a lack of acquaintance with Christianity which seems incomprehensible in the light of the facts to which we have just pointed. It is not until one of the latest Meccan Suras that he mentions Jesus, or Isa, as he is called in the Koran, the name being apparently derived from the form Isho, which was prevalent among the Nestorians. As to the place of the person of Jesus in Christianity, in Mecca he only knew that the Christians called Jesus the Son of God. Moreover, he confused the mother of Jesus with Aaron's sister Miriam, and thus at first he seems to have regarded Jesus as an Old Testament prophet. He knew nothing at all about the Christian doctrine of the sacraments, or the

[1] Braun, O., *Moses bar Kepha*, p. 145.

Christian cult, with its festivals and its hierarchical system. It can hardly be assumed that his silence on these matters was due to his being interested in Christianity only in so far as it agreed with his own beliefs. When he did learn something concerning the main doctrine of Christianity—namely, the divinity of Jesus—probably through his close connections with Christian Abyssinia—he vigorously attacked it as polytheism. This also applies to the Trinity, which he thought consisted of God, Jesus, and Mary, and in his opinion such a doctrine was genuine polytheism. Mohammed cannot have had permanent personal relations with Christians who had accurate information concerning their religion. What he did learn about Christianity in the course of time—amongst other things, fragments of the legends of Jesus and his mother, from the apocryphal Gospels—was apparently obtained from persons whose religious knowledge was extremely incomplete.

On the other hand, we have seen that the Prophet was not only acquainted with the main outlines of the Christian doctrines of judgment, retribution, and good works, but also that he reproduced in detail the interpretations of these doctrines which were prevalent in the churches of the Orient, and at times he even employs a style[1] and expressions which must have had a Christian origin. This riddle can be solved only in one way. At some time Mohammed must have heard a Christian missionary sermon. As I have tried to prove in an earlier work on the origin of Islam, one often notices in Mohammed's revelations a fixed rhetorical scheme with approximately the following outline: (1) A description of the blessings of God as revealed in His providence, especially in the wonderful creation of man, and the life-giving rain which brings about productive growth for the nourishment of man. (2) The duty of man, therefore, to serve God alone in faith and good works. (3) The judgment and retribution which shall come upon all who do not fulfil this duty. Ever since the days of the Christian apostles this has been the prevailing style of Christian missionary preaching. We know

[1] Comp. Andrae, *Ursprung des Islams* K.H.A., 1925, pp. 70 ff.

that none of the Oriental churches carried on so active a missionary programme as did the Nestorians, who established important Christian churches in Central Asia, India, and China. It is not overbold to assume that Nestorian monks from the Arabian churches in Mesopotamia, or from Nejran in Yemen after the Persians had conquered this country in 597, in the course of their preaching tours among their pagan countrymen, visited Hejaz, with whose capital city the Christian Arabs maintained a lively contact. As a matter of fact, tradition tells of a Christian preacher named Quss ibn Sa'ida, who is said to have been Bishop of Nejran, but who belonged to a tribe living at Hira in Mesopotamia, whom Mohammed is supposed to have heard preaching in the market at Ukaz.[1]

The word falls by the wayside and upon stony ground. But when it finds a receptive spirit its power is often greater than we are able to comprehend. The message which Mohammed heard concerning the one God, His goodness, and His judgment, took root in his soul. Many years passed; the outward conditions and the associations in which the message reached him faded from his memory; but the word lived. Unrealized by him, its innermost meaning, the creative energy of its ideas, became Mohammed's personal spiritual possession. It was intensified by what he heard from time to time concerning the Christian hermits and itinerant preachers, who also occasionally passed through Hejaz. And it is part of the mystery of the inspiration of the Prophet and of the poet, that the power which these ideas wielded over his soul was never fully clear to him until, like a revelation from above, they emerged in a new form of unsurmised and incomprehensible clarity and consistency. No more than other inspired men could Mohammed recognize his own reminiscences and ideas in this new form.

It was obvious to the Prophet that his message was not unrelated to the faith of cultured peoples, the Jews and the

[1] *Kitab al-aghani*, xiv, pp. 41 ff.; Abu Nu'aim, *Dala'il al-nubuwwa*, Hyderabad, 1320, p. 28 f.; Mas'udi, i, p. 33.

Christians. The revelation which came to him contained the same features that may be found in their sacred scriptures. He was therefore interested in gaining a better knowledge of their religion. Faith is a conviction of things not seen. But at first he did not despise the confirmation of experience. Hence he was not a traitor to his faith or to his prophetic call, nor is it a proof of a subtle and premeditated plan that Mohammed should have continuously attempted to question Jews and Christians about their religion. Various passages in the Koran indicate that Mohammed's pagan opponents did not hesitate to expose his dependence upon others, and to assert, naturally not without a certain justification, that the content of his revelation really came from external authorities. 'And the infidels say, "This Koran is a mere fraud of his own devising, and others have helped him with it" . . . And they say, "Tales of the ancients that he hath put in writing! (or caused to be put in writing) and they were dictated to him morn and even"' (Sura 25, 5-6). At times the accusations pointed toward a specific person, a man of alien nationality who had only a poor command of the Arabic tongue: 'We know also that they say, "Surely a certain person teacheth him." But the tongue of him at whom they hint is foreign, while this Koran is in plain Arabic' (16, 105). Henry Lammens has proved that there were several Christians in Mecca, especially black slaves and legionaries from Ethiopia, as well as labourers and traders from Syria. But apart from a few Biblical narratives these simple Christians could not have told him much about their own faith. And what they did have to tell did not undermine the Prophet's conviction that in all essentials his belief was identical with theirs. They were not able to expose the defects of the system which he erected, or to shake his religious self-confidence. It was otherwise when Mohammed became acquainted in Medina with a congregation which possessed a certain measure of scriptural learning and religious training. There he was forced to wage a battle of life and death with the Jews, to vindicate his belief in his prophetic call.

CHAPTER IV

Mohammed's Doctrine of Revelation

MOHAMMED 'did not expect that the Book would be given to him' (Sura 28, 86). He was not conscious that he had even entertained so bold a desire as the wish to be the prophet of his people, and present to the Arabs a holy scripture such as the Jews and Christians possessed. When for the first time he heard the voice of the angel speaking the divine words in his ear, it was to him an unexpected, incomprehensible marvel. The whole assurance of his 'call,' the faith which supported him amidst derision and persecution, which led him with confidence to defy both men and demons to produce a similarly marvellous Koran, is based on this moment of surprise—a phenomenon well known to us from the experiences of prophets, mediums, and ecstatics.

He was conscious of no premeditation. Does this mean that none such was present? Assuredly not. The spirit of inspiration does not function in a vacuum. It employs the assembled material that the soul already possesses, whether actually in the consciousness or hidden and concealed in the dark subconscious. Thus it is that inspiration, which is so clearly unrelated to any personal wishes or expectations, in general adapts its form to those ideas which are particularly prominent in the environment concerned. If it is usual for it to take the form of possession, whereby a spirit speaks through the medium's mouth, then a new prophet appears as one possessed. If an ecstatic, visionary journey to heaven is the normal mode of connection with the unseen world, then the inspirational experience will inevitably take this form. Particularly among people of a primitive culture, inspirational experiences almost always, among the same people, follow a uniform type. It would seem as though this type hovers, as it were, above the mental process, as a formative principle, so soon as revelation begins to operate. It is more than probable that the form assumed by Mohammed's presentation of his prophetic revelation was determined in advance by the thoughts—and why not also by the secret desires?—which had dwelt in his mind through years of anticipation.

Belief in the judgment and everlasting punishment was the religious motive for Mohammed's appearance, and fixed the content of his revelation. Yet as far as its essential content goes this belief need not have found expression in a prophetic revelation. Mohammed might have become a Christian, or his awakening might have incited him to seek to live a pious and ascetic life in accordance with the demands of Christian monasticism, such as he had come to know it. Why did he not do this? The reason is to be sought in certain fixed ideas concerning holy scriptures and divine revelation, which Mohammed must have embraced long before his own call.

Disquietude and anxiety arising from thoughts of Allah's judgment had driven him to meditate in solitude. Conscience admitted the stern claims of the Judge. He desired earnestly to walk in the path of righteousness so far as he knew it. The Christian ascetics and monks, whose revivalist sermons had touched his heart, had also made a deep impression on him by their severe devotional exercises. In the stillness of the night, while men of the world, forgetful of judgment and eternity, were sleeping soundly, the pious were awake. They stood praying with outstretched arms; they bowed down or fell prostrate on the ground; and all the time one could hear their incessant murmuring or their singsong recitation. He knew that the words which they muttered in a foreign tongue came from their holy scriptures, and he believed that the essential thing about this devotional exercise, its religious efficacy, resided wholly in the reading of the holy text. So how could he, Mohammed, pray correctly if he had no holy scripture to read? He could not use the scriptures of Jews or Christians, because they were written in a foreign language.

It clearly did not occur to Mohammed that they might be translated. Thus for him and his fellow-countrymen an Arabic Holy Scripture was necessary above all things.

Mohammed knew that the record of revelation consisted of a book or collection of books. The Jews and Christians he was wont to call 'literate folk,' People of the Book. Nevertheless, he himself did not think of revelation as a written record which the pious man might read for himself in private devotion. He thought of the reading of scripture in Divine Service or prayer, of the lection which was often recited from memory during the vigils of the ascetics. That he had so dreamed and desired is clear to us from the fact that no sooner did the voice of the angel speak to his ear the solemn, divine words than he identified them as a 'reading.' The word used in the Syrian Church for the scripture reading in Divine Service, *qeryana,* Mohammed took and applied as a title to his revelation. He likewise called each individual revelation a Koran, as well as the revelation in its entirety, and so he called the portion of revelation that is read in every devotional exercise. For Mohammed the record of revelation is not the writing down of a closed sacred history or tradition, and in particular it is not something eternal and unchangeable. It is the proclamation of Allah's favours and the thanklessness of men, the announcement of judgment and recompense, Allah's warning to the faithful of this world, and His guidance to right belief and conduct. His conception of scripture is dynamic, not static. Scripture is not given to mankind once for all in a fixed, unalterable form, and so every people may rightly lay claim to share the awakening and guidance which scripture gives. For this reason every people has its scripture and its prophet. The various records of revelation in their spiritual sense and aim fully agree with one another. Each scripture confirms the others. Jesus confirmed the revelation that came to Moses, and Mohammed confirmed the revelation that had earlier been given to Jews and Christians. The true believer recognizes all these different revelations as sent from God. 'Say, we believe in Allah, and in what has been revealed to us, in what was revealed to Abraham, Ishmael, Isaac, Jacob, and the tribes; in what was given to Moses and Jesus, and in what the prophets received from their lord: we make no distinction between any of them' (2, 130). Nevertheless, this does not mean that one community must adapt itself in all things to the manners and customs of the others. Allah has on good grounds given particular ordinances to different peoples. To the Jews, as a special punishment for their obstinacy, and love of provoking opposition, which had given Mohammed so many painful hours in Medina, He had proclaimed a prohibition against eating the flesh of many animals that in themselves are clean and good. Mohammed had a very liberal conception of ritual prescriptions. Such are not grounded in any eternal Divine necessity, but are only the appropriate regulations which Allah has given the various peoples according to their needs.

So Mohammed's mission means that he has come with scripture and guidance to a people 'who had hitherto received no Warner'; that the Arab people, who up till now seemed to have been forgotten by Allah, has now also received its book, 'a clear Arabic Koran,' and now stands forth as having equal rights with the People of the Book. This conception of a revelation, uniform in all its essential content, which, in a form suitable to their particular needs, has been given to each people in its own peculiar language, is such a curious theological conception that one can hardly believe that Mohammed, whose strength certainly did not lie in the realm of theological speculation, could have evolved it himself. Nor can one maintain that it must have arisen out of the religious *milieu* that preceded Mohammed. The Arabs, a people without a Book and without a prophet, were, it is true, surrounded by peoples who did read sacred scriptures, but Mohammed must have learned, particularly from Christianity, that its unity was religious, not national. In his native town Mohammed might have encountered Copts, Abyssinians, Syrians, and perhaps also Greeks, and so could not have been in ignorance of the fact that the Christians in Abyssinia spoke a different tongue from those in Syria, and yet had the same scripture, the 'Gospel,' as Mohammed calls it. The historical situation, of which he must have been aware, was also at variance with his theological formula, that each people had received its revelation in its own proper language.

The Arabian prophet cannot have received his doctrine of revelation from Judaism, nor from the Orthodox Christian Church. The conception of prophecy as something living and actual, something that could belong to the present and to the future, could hardly, so far as I can see, have arisen in Mohammed's soul if he had known nothing more of prophets and prophecy than was taught by Judaism and the Christian churches in the Orient. Mohammed knew of the Jewish expectation of the coming Messiah. He knew that a prophet was promised in the Torah, and linked this prophecy with Jesus' promise that he would send the Comforter. For him, this belief in a Messiah provided a support for his conviction of his call, but he cannot have invented it. No trace of this belief, however, can be found in Mohammed's conception of revelation. Rather he remoulded the Messianic hope in accordance with his ideas of prophecy. In the Christian Church the voices of the early Christian 'prophets' had long since fallen silent. Their successors among the pious monks, who were usually called *pneumatics*—'the spiritual ones'—who received visionary revelations, and were able to read, prophetically, the thoughts of men, have nothing in common with the Koranic notions about prophets. Nor does it avail anything to cite the fact that theological writers such as Cyril of Jerusalem count among the prophets as well as the prophets of Scripture such saints of Biblical history as Abraham, Isaac, Jacob, Joseph, and Moses, who also take their place among the prophets of the Koran. The significant thing about Mohammed is just this, that he excludes the *writing* prophets. Above all, note that these personalities all belonged to the past. The common belief was that they belonged to a class which was exalted far above the sphere of humanity. An Oriental Christian of the seventh century would as soon have dreamed of becoming a partriarch or an angel as of becoming a prophet like those of the Bible. Moreover, the idea of a particular revelation for each people is entirely foreign to the Christian doctrine.

Syria, where the advancing Greek culture encountered Babylonian astral cults and Persian mythology, has been of special importance in the history of ancient religious syncretism. Peculiar religious sects and religio-philosophic teachings, in which Greek thought endeavoured to classify and clarify the mythological learning to the East, had one after another started from this area on a longer or shorter triumphal march towards the West. Moreover, the remains of the primitive Christian community in Palestine, which shortly before the destruction of Jerusalem had emigrated to the region of the east of the Jordan, was quickly influenced by this heathen thought-world, with its alluring mystical teaching. Here, at an early date, we find a peculiar doctrine of revelation. In the Gospel of the Hebrews which was utilized by these Judaeo-Christian sects, it is said, concerning the baptism of Jesus: 'As the Lord came up out of the water, there came down the whole fount of the Holy Spirit and rested on him, and said to him, "In all the prophets I awaited thee till thou shouldst come, that I might find my resting place in thee, for thou art my resting place, my first-born Son, who reignest for ever."' Thus, according to the Gospel of the Hebrews, one and the same divine Being, the fount of the Holy Spirit, had taken form in all the prophets, or had inspired them, until finally it had found in Christ its full and definite revelation. This reminds one of the portrayal of the Wisdom of God in the apocryphal Book of Wisdom, a picture that is coloured by the Stoic philosophy. Wisdom, which is the goodliest, most active, and purest of all things, and which therefore, like the World Reason of the Stoics, permeates all, is a reflection of the eternal light, and mirrors back the works of God. 'From generation to generation it flows in pious souls, and maketh men God's friends and prophets.'[1] This notion encountered in the East a Persian doctrine of a divine Saviour and Guide, the Heavenly Man, who once in the beginning showed helpless man the way of truth and life, and who will reveal Himself once again as Redeemer and the procreator of truth.

Epiphanius[2] explains that Ebion, the alleged founder of the Judaeo-Christian sect, but more probably one of its supporters, held that Christ was Adam, the first man to be created by God, and into whom God breathed His breath. The Heavenly Man, the first Adam, used now and then to come down from His supra-mundane life, assume a visible form and appear to the patriarchs. 'After He had come thus to Abraham, Isaac, and Jacob, in the last days He came clothed in the body of the same Adam. He appeared as a man, was crucified, rose again, and went to heaven.' The heavenly Christ was thus actually incarnated twice and lived twice on earth—in Adam and in Christ. But He had often assumed an occasional and visible form, and had thus revealed himself to the most distinguished saints of the Old Testament.

A peculiar vacillation between these two different conceptions is characteristic of this Judaeo-Christian doctrine of revelation. First the heavenly messenger and helper, Adam-Christ, is conceived of as dwelling in the prophets and men of God and assuming human form in them. Then it is said that only twice, at the beginning and at the end of the world-period, did He assume human form, and, moreover, showed Himself only to holy persons whom He had found worthy of divine instruction. The first conception corresponds more with the Judaeo-Greek idea of the spirit of wisdom and revelation which descended upon the prophets and dwelt in them. The second belongs to the Oriental doctrine of a Redeemer who from His high kingdom may occasionally reveal Himself to the elect, but who actually came only twice into this mundane world.

[1] Wisdom, vii.
[2] Haer. xxx, 3.

One advocate of this doctrine of revelation is the mystic prophet Elxai, who appeared in the country to the east of the Jordan in the third year of the reign of the Emperor Trajan. Elxai—the name is in reality a title and means 'the hidden power'—had once seen in a vision a gigantic angel twenty miles high, and beside him a female being 'standing like a statue above the clouds between two hills.' According to the revelation which Elxai received from the angel, Christ was a being who had often been born on the earth. At different times He had assumed different forms and had entered many bodies. Sometimes He was born of a virgin mother, and at other times in the usual way. Sometimes He came 'as spirit.' The Christ had thus at times allowed Himself to be born in human form, and at times had bestowed revelation on the prophets as a spiritual being.[1] Elxai's idea of his own position as a prophet seems peculiar. According to Epiphanius[2] the cloud-high angel was none other than the heavenly Christ. The woman beside Him was the Holy Spirit. Spirit, as is well known, is feminine in the Aramaic tongue. Elxai was thereby satisfied that he was one of those who could receive instruction and revelation from the heavenly messenger. But his remarkable name denotes yet something more. 'The Hidden Power' reminds one of the name which the Samaritan prophet, Simon the Magus, gave himself—'the great power of God.' Actually this name means that Simon believed that he was an incarnation of the eternal Christ.

Similar ideas are prominent in the Pseudo-Clementine writings. All wisdom and knowledge, and above all, knowledge of the way of salvation, God had imparted from eternity to the heavenly Christ, the 'Prophet of Truth,' the 'Son of God,' the 'Prince of men.' He knows all: the past as it was, the present as it is, the future as it will be. For with the eye of the soul, which knows no limitations, He comprehends and understands secret things. He does not possess the spirit only at certain times, when the rapture comes upon Him,

[1] Hippolytus ix, 4; x, 29.
[2] Haer. xix, 4.

as is the case with ordinary prophets, but He has a special innate endowment which never dries up.[1] This Prophet of the Truth is identical with Adam, the father of the human race, who was formed by the very hand of God, and who finally became man a second time in Jesus.[2] To assert that Adam sinned against God is contrary to the truth and an insult to the eternal King whose image he is. In His own person he has thus appeared only twice. Nevertheless, He has at different times chosen men, whom he found to be pure, as his prophets. Thus He revealed himself to Abraham, Moses, and other saints of the Old Testament.[3] Epiphanius mentions Abraham, Isaac, Jacob, Moses, Aaron, and Joshua as prophets of the Ebionites. On the other hand, Isaiah, Jeremiah, and the other prophets of Scripture were excluded.[4] That is to say, the Old Testament, according to the teaching of the Clementines, has been interpolated by false prophets, who smuggled in stories of sins and errors that Adam and the pious patriarchs were alleged to have committed, and asserted that God takes pleasure in wars and bloody sacrifices.

The doctrine of revelation which we have here described was likely formulated more or less clearly by the Sethians,[5] among whom were the Gnostic Justinus, who counted one prophet of the heathen, viz. Hercules, among the body of 'sent ones,'[6] and the Syrian Bar Daisan, who before his conversion had been a priest in a temple of Atargatis, and who taught that Christ had appeared to Abraham and the other prophets in a heavenly body, and talked with them, until finally he took on bodily form through the Virgin Mary.[7] According to Arabic sources Bar Daisan held that

[1] Clem., *Hom.* ii, 6; iii, 11, 13.

[2] Clem., *Recogn.* i, 47. Waitz, *Die Pseudoklementinen,* 126, n. 3

[3] Yet there often appears an idea reminding us of the Gospel of the Hebrews and Wisdom vii. The Prophet of Truth passes down through the ages, changing name and form, until he finds "rest." *Hom.* iii, 17; *Recogn.* i, 28, 33, 34.

[4] Haer. xxx, 18.

[5] Haer. xxxix, 1.

[6] Hippolytus v, 26.

[7] A. Hahn, *Bardesanes gnosticus,* p. 85; Burkitt, *Early Eastern Christianity,* p. 160.

'Allah's light had descended into his heart.'[1] He thus considered himself to be the prophet of the Christ-Being, or perhaps indeed his incarnation.

These ideas received a notable exposition at the hands of Mani, the preacher and martyr, who in the year 276 was crucified by the Persian king Bahram I at the city gate of Gundeshapur. By his profound theosophic speculation; by his poetical talents, well suited to the fantastic Oriental myths, whereby he contrived to utilize them as a medium for a religio-philosophical system; by a grave ascetic piety and a keen faculty for organization, he had, before this event, succeeded in calling into being a speculative religious movement which became of far-reaching importance. According to the Arabic writer, Ibn an-Nadim, Mani in his twelfth year had received a revelation from the King of the Paradise of Light. When he was twenty-four years old the angel at-Tawwam came to him—the name is Nabataean and means 'companion'—and said: 'Greetings to thee, Mani, from me and from the Lord who has sent me to thee, and has chosen thee to be His messenger.'[2] Another Arabic writer, al-Biruni, gives us an important citation from one of the actual writings of Mani. 'From time to time messengers from God have come with wisdom and pious works. In one generation they came through an apostle named Buddha to the land of India, in another through Zoroaster to Persia, in a third through Jesus to the West. This prophetic office has now, in this best of generations, come through me, Mani, the apostle of the God of truth, to the land of Babel.'[3] Besides those mentioned, Mani recognized also Adam, Seth, Noah, and Abraham as prophets.[4] A heavenly being of light, who bears the mystic names 'the third Messenger,' 'Jesus,' 'the Virgin of Light,' took shape in these prophets or revealed himself to them. On this point we find the same peculiar obscurity in Mani

[1] Al-Biruni, ed. Sachau, p. 207.
[2] Fihrist, ed. Flügel, p. 328.
[3] Al-Biruni, p. 207.
[4] Augustine, *Contra Faustum*, xix, 3.

which we have already encountered in his predecessors. The fact that the heavenly revealer of God seems at one time to be identified with His messengers and prophets and at another to be distinguished from them has from the beginning given rise to difficulties for Christian polemists.[1] In the person of Jesus there clearly appears an earthly revelation of the Heavenly Messenger himself. Jesus was no ordinary man. What the Christians relate about Jesus' birth, circumcision, temptation in the wilderness, and such-like things, which disparage his divine dignity, are false. The Jesus whom the Jews crucified was thus not the Heavenly One, who, thanks to His supernatural nature, cannot suffer. It was another being, who is sometimes called a demon, and sometimes the 'son of the widow,' whom God put in His place. Mani himself seems at times to wish to proclaim himself only a human messenger. He has received a visit from the 'companion,' who indeed is no other than the Heavenly Messenger. He calls himself humbly 'a grateful disciple from the land of Babylon.'[2] He is the apostle of Jesus that is, the messenger of the Heavenly Revealer of God.[3] On the other hand, however, it is affirmed that Mani gave himself out as an apostle of Christ,[4] of his very nature, as the Comforter, the Holy Spirit whom Jesus had promised, and as Christ himself.[5] In the Manichaean texts from Turfan, in numerous hymns and prayers, Jesus, the Virgin of Light, and the Lord Mani, are brought together in such a way as to make it clear that

[1] "Have you Manichees three different Christs?" asks Augustine (*Contr. Faust*, xii, 11), and Epiphanius (*Haer.* xix, 3) is not always able rightly to understand whether what Elxai says about Christ really refers to our Lord and Saviour.

[2] *Hymnus*, tr. Lidzbarski, *Nach. der Gesell. d. Wiss.*, Göttingen, 1918, p. 501.

[3] For references see Schaeder, *Urform and Fortbildung des manichäischen Systems*, Vorträge der Bibl. Warburg, iv, 129; cf. also Waldschmidt and Lenz, *Die Stellung Jesu im manichäischen System*, Abhand. d. Preuss Akad. d. Wiss., 1926, p. 59.

[4] Addai Scher, *Histoire Nestorienne*, P.O. iv, 228.

[5] Eusebius, *Hist. Eccl.* vii, 31, 1; cf. "Bibliographie Manichéenne," J.A., 1911, p. 505, 1913, p. 99.

the same person is meant,[1] and in the Chinese texts he is called Buddha.[2] Either, it may be, Mani himself, in preaching to the initiated, had given them to understand that he was not only the apostle of the eternal Christ, but Christ himself in a visible form, or the later Manichaean community had raised their founder and prophet to the sphere of the divine.

We have seen that Mani did not limit revelation to the group of Biblical worthies. This idea, which appears also in Justinus and the Sethians, he made one of the fundamental ideas of this theory of revelation. The message came at different times to different peoples. The great religions of the West, of India and Persia, contain one and the same Divine wisdom; their founders are all messengers of God. Mani takes it to be his particular vocation to point out wherein this common element in Christianity, Mazdaism, and Buddhism consists.

This doctrine relating to the messenger and prophet of truth had not, so far as we know, called forth any new prophet later than Mani and before Mohammed. But the idea lived on. In the tenth century Ibn an-Nadim still found in Mesopotamia 'Sabians' who appear to have accepted doctrines of the kind here described. Syrian bishops encountered heretics with similar ideas during their visitations in the regions about the Arabian desert.[3] Manichaeism, which was so powerful in Central Asia, and had extended its influence from the boundaries of China to the heart of Europe, would certainly not have been unknown in a city with so lively a commerce as Mecca. Arabic chroniclers, indeed, report that Zindiqs—i.e. probably Manichaeans—had come from al-Hira to Mecca.[4]

The Byzantine religious policy soon constrained the few adherents of the old Gnostic sects, as well as the vigorous Manichaean Mission, to observe great prudence in lands where

[1] Alfaric, *Les Ecritures manichéennes*, ii, 13, n. 2; cf. also *J.R.A.S.*, 1920, p. 2.

[2] Schaeder, p. 103.

[3] Assemani, *Bibl. Orient*, iii, 2, pp. 482, 609, 614.

[4] Ibn Rosteh, *Kitab al-A'laq an-Naffsa*, ed. de Goeje, *B.G.A.* vii, 217.

Christianity was dominant. Mazdaism was also openly hostile to the life-blighting asceticism of Mani. Moreover, in these circles it was early regarded as permissible to conceal one's real faith, if circumstances made it necessary. On heathen soil it was possible to proceed with greater freedom. In this connection, a peculiarity which must have drawn particular attention to these often fanatically intractable heretics was their proud abandonment of the Christian churches. Whether they considered Jesus himself as a prophet among the prophets or frankly considered him as identical with the Heavenly Messenger operating in all ages, they daringly accused the Church of having in respect of definite points falsified true religion. In particular, the notion that all religions, especially those that were able to name a personal founder, contained the same eternal truth, must have given a vigorous boost to the national pride of the heathen peoples. The claim of Christianity, as of Judaism, to be the sole true religion had always appeared to them as a wrongful and provocative presumption. The more the old folk-religions of the Orient began to decline, while Christianity forged ahead on different fronts, not only as a religious force, but also as the triumphant bearer of a higher culture, the more bitter the sense of enmity must have grown. One may compare the way in which, in modern India, the theosophical proclamation of the similar truth-value of all the higher religions has incited, among the coloured peoples, the prevailing discontent with the political and cultural tutelage of the whites.

It is clear that Mohammed must have been influenced, even if he was not actually awakened, by the struggle for religious independence which had given Mani and the Gnostics such a strong position among the peoples of the Orient. The serious spiritual awakening due to the preaching of the judgment by wandering Syrian preachers had given content and direction to his faith; the belief in revelation gave its peculiar form to his religious consciousness. He can hardly have come into personal contact with the adherents of these Gnostic sects. Of their doctrinal system he knew little or nothing.

He had merely got hold of the ideas which had immediate relevance for the religious position in which he found himself. So we now understand why he, as far as we can see, never even gave a thought to the possibility of becoming a Christian. He already knew, from the echo of the Gnostic-Manichaean theory of revelation which had reached his ears, that Christendom was only one among other similarly privileged communities which had experienced Divine guidance and revelation. Further, he knew—and this idea struck deeper root in his soul than any other—that every people had its prophet. Where was the man who would bring revelation to his people? This thought, combined perhaps with what he had himself witnessed during a *qeryana* of the hermits in their devout recitation of psalms and other holy texts, was the creative idea which prepared the way for the revelation of the angel, and his dictation out of the holy book. To imagine that the revelation came first—and Mohammed's conception of his call was only an interpretation of the experience of the inspiration which had already occurred—does away with any possibility of explaining the matter psychologically. That the conscious appropriation and clear formulation of the prophetic conception of the 'call' grew only gradually and slowly is merely what we had every reason to expect.

Mohammed's conception of revelation thus betrays a relationship to the Ebionitic-Manichaean doctrine which cannot be accidental. The case is otherwise with regard to the external *form* of the revelation. As to *how* the heavenly messenger communicated with the prophet of a people, this teaching, so far as Mohammed knew of it, said nothing. Yet even here his unconsciously working fancy did not act, nor could it act, in an absolute vacuum. His notions as to how inspiration actually occurred he had to take from the single form of actual inspiration which he knew from his own experience—namely, that of the soothsayers and poets of his own people. His heathen countrymen soon discovered that the new prophet was akin to a *kahin* or a poet. The voice of an invisible being dictated the revelation in his ear, and his Koran was composed in the same oracular, solemn, doggerel verses as the utterances of the soothsayers.

Finally, there is not lacking external testimony that a real connection existed between the earliest Islam and these Gnostic sects. Mohammed's followers were frequently—and precisely in the historically valuable tradition of the old stories of the prophet's war-like expeditions—called 'Sabians' by his opponents, a word which was the common name for a group of the sects here mentioned. This title cannot have come from the Koran. The Sabians are there mentioned on a few occasions as a particular community which differed from the Christians and Muslims. It is in the highest degree improbable that the tradition of this nickname has no real foundation. So we may take it that in Mecca it was clear that the teaching of Mohammed had a certain relationship with that of the Sabians.

A peculiar religious term which Mohammed employed in Medina, and in the later years at Mecca—namely, the expression *Hanif*—probably points in the same direction. In the Meccan Suras the word denotes 'monotheist,' and is used in contradistinction to 'the idol-worshippers' (98, 4; 22, 32; 10, 105). In Sura 30, 29 it is pointed out that this belief in a single God is the natural religion which corresponds to the God-given predisposition of mankind. 'So direct they countenance to religion as a *Hanif*, in accordance with those God-given predispositions which He has given man. Allah's creation cannot be altered. This is the true religion.' During the later period in Mecca, and above all in Medina, the word *Hanif* is generally employed in reference to Abraham, where Mohammed particularly emphasizes the fact that 'Abraham was neither a Jew nor a Christian, but a *Hanif*, a Muslim, one who did not belong to the idol-worshippers' (3, 60; 2, 129). Since Abraham is thus represented as a *Hanif*, Mohammed must clearly have had two ideas in mind. Although both the religions of Scripture count him among their men of God, Abraham was neither a Jew nor a Christian, but a monotheist who had cut himself off from the worship of idols. The Gospel and the Torah, as Mohammed emphasizes, were sent long after the time of Abraham. Thus the people of the Book had no right to claim him for themselves. Further, according to the Koranic legend, Abraham, who lived amidst an idol-worshipping people, had by simple meditation come to see the vanity and impotency of the heathen idols. The star to which the people pray is setting; he sees this, and comprehends that a god who is evanescent cannot be the all-seeing, true God. He discovers that the images of the gods cannot defend themselves if anyone breaks them in pieces; still less can they help anyone else. So one may say that Abraham followed the 'God-given predisposition,' the instinct for believing in the one true God which is implanted in every human soul.

Hanif thus means for Mohammed a monotheist—in the majority of cases where the word is used, he adds "not one of the idol-worshippers'—who is yet neither Jew nor Christian, who attaches himself to none of the existing religious communities, and who by his own investigation and meditation has gained an insight into the comparative worthlessness of heathenism.

The Arabic word comes doubtless from the Syriac *hanpa*, meaning 'heathen.' How then came the word 'heathen' to have in the Koran the sense of 'monotheist'? It is used in the Syriac Bible of heathen in general, and in ecclesiastical language for Greek heathenism in particular. Thus, for example, Julian the Apostate is called *Yulyana hanpa*. The Christian Syrians did not use the word for heretics in general, but only for those whose standpoint approximated so nearly to that of Hellenic heathendom that they could be reckoned as apostates from the Christian religion. Thus Mani's teaching is plainly called *hanputa*, heathenism. The Sabians, it is true, are first called 'heathen' in works that were written after the Arabic conquest, but everything suggests that they were known as 'heathen' at a much earlier date.

If Manichaeans and Sabians were thus directly called *hanpe*, 'heathen,' we can understand how the word could gradually come to mean, in Arabic, a monotheist who is neither a Jew nor a Christian. Mohammed, however, seems to understand by the term *hanif* rather a man who, without belonging to a definite religious community, yet spontaneously, directed only by the 'God-given predisposition,' has separated himself from the popular heathenism. Hence we must assume that the struggle for religious independence, and the belief in a general monotheistic religion, revealed to all peoples, which came from the Manichaean and Syrian *hanpe*, did not, in Mohammed's time, so far as he was aware, originate in direct connection with these sects, but rather as a feeling after a new independent religion, free from the idol-worship of heathenism, and not bound by any Jewish or Christian rites or laws—and thus a religion to which one could swear allegiance without having to sacrifice national distinctiveness and independence, such as one would have to do on joining a foreign religious community (*umma*). The leading thought of the Manichaean movement had thus detached itself from the sphere of the sect itself, and had wandered far beyond its borders. As scientific doctrines and philosphical and political ideas which have penetrated the masses and lost all indication of their origin may yet be recognized as an anonymous tendency in general thought, so the old Gnostic doctrine of revelation appears to have operated in Arabia. Perhaps it called forth more experiments in the direction of providing the longed-for Arabian religion of revelation than that of Mohammed. The rival prophets who appeared during Mohammed's later years were, it is true, inspired by his example. But in the case of one of them, Musailimah in Yemen, the question may be asked whether he had not already appeared while Mohammed was still only an unknown quantity in Mecca.

What Islamic tradition relates concerning the *Hanifs*, who forsook the heathen customs of their people and sought a better religion, bears a markedly legendary stamp. At a sacrificial feast which the Quraish held for one of their idols, four men, so Ibn Ishak relates,[1] separated themselves from the people in order to seek the true Hanifitic religion, the faith of Abraham. These four were Waraka bin Naufal, Ubaidallah bin Jahsh, Uthman bin al-Huwairith, and Zeid bin Amr. Waraka became a Christian, and acquired much knowledge from the Christians, and out of their books. Ubaidallah remained in doubt and uncertainty until he accepted Islam, and emigrated to Abyssinia. There he went over to Christianity, and proudly explained to his earlier co-religionists: 'We see clearly, but you are still blinking like newly born puppies.' Uthman betook himself to the ruler of Byzantium, there became a Christian, and occupied an honourable position at Court. Zeid became neither Jew nor Christian. He kept himself from idolatry and from eating flesh which had been sacrificed to the idols, and upbraided his people for their false idol-worship. As he prayed at the Ka'ba he said: 'My God, if I knew what form of worship is most pleasing to Thee I would choose it, but I know it not.' The Prophet said of him: 'On the last day Zeid will rise up, a community in himself.'

Although the story of the *Hanifs* is from beginning to end a fanciful elaboration of certain indications found in the Koran, one has nevertheless a distinct impression that what is told of these four men, who are expressly named, and their different histories, was not wholly without a foundation of fact. It is noteworthy that three of the four became Christians. Legend could hardly have invented such a conversion of pious men who sought the true doctrine of Abraham. Rather would it have made them adherents of Mohammed and witnesses to the truth of Islam. On the other hand, it fits in nicely with our theory that the tendency which the *Hanifs* represent came originally from the Christian sects. Perhaps it is no accident that the *Hanifs* are specially represented as turning away from the heathen cult and above all from bloody sacrifices. It reminds us of the violent attacks on bloody sacrifices, even those of the Old Testament, in the

[1] Ibn Hisham, 120.

Clementine writings, and also in Manichaism, which forbade not only animal sacrifices, but killing in general.

One of the four, Waraka bin Naufal, has been brought by Islamic tradition into connection with Mohammed's first appearance. When the prophet was uneasy and distressed, and felt uncertain as to how he should take the revelation which he had received, Khadijah sent messengers to her cousin Waraka. This man, who had studied the Christian scriptures, comforted her by saying: 'This is verily the great *namus* which came to Moses.' From the context it is not quite clear whether the word *namus*, the Greek *nomos*, law, is to be understood as a person or as a revealed writing. The Clementines speak of the eternal *nomos* that came to Moses and to the other prophets.[1] Now has legend merely invented this story of Waraka in order to produce from the mysterious wisdom of the People of the Book a proof of Mohammed's divine mission? In that case it would rather have been a priest or a monk who would have appeared in the story. For this reason I consider it probable that the story of Waraka conceals an actual reminiscence of a connection between the new religion and the seekers for monotheism in the last years of heathenism. So I suggest that this relation of Khadijah's had already spoken with Mohammed about the great *namus* before the day on which the angel came with his call.

For the rest, definite traces of Manichaean teaching can be found only in one single particular: namely Mohammed's peculiar notion concerning the death of Jesus. 'The Jews say, "Verily we have killed the Messiah, Jesus the Son of Mary, the Apostle of God," but he was neither killed nor crucified by them; he merely appeared so to them. . . . Really, indeed, they did not kill him, but God took him up to Himself' (4, 156). Mohammed does not believe, with the usual Gnostic Docetism, that Jesus himself suffered in a false body, but obviously, like Mani, and before him Basilides, that an-

[1] Andrae, *Ursprung des Islams*, p. 110.

other person took his place and was crucified by the Jews.[1] Thus at any rate the Muslim exegetes of the oldest period understood it.[2] They relate that of his own free will one of Jesus' disciples took it upon himself to suffer for his Master, and was made by God to resemble him, so that the Jews believed that they had crucified Jesus himself; or that it was Judas who as punishment for his treachery had to die in Jesus' stead.

May one venture to seek here an interpretation of the enigmatical name, 'the son of the widow,' which Mani gave to Jesus? As Ibn an—Nadim explains,[3] Mani believed 'that Jesus whom we and the Christians revere was a devil.' This is a re-echoed version of the bitter polemic which purposely distorted Mani's teaching, that a demon had been put to death upon the cross in the place of Jesus, into the assertion that Mani had called Jesus a devil. Just so the 'son of the widow,' with whom a special chapter of the Book of Mysteries deals,[4] is, according to Mani's idea, in no way identical with the 'historical Jesus.' He is the person who was crucified in his stead. Thus in all probability Mani, like the exegetes of Islam, taught a double doctrine concerning the substitute at the crucifixion—he was either a demon or a miscreant who was crucified as a punishment, or one of the faithful, a disciple who died of his own free will. Who may this unknown disciple have been? It is no far-fetched supposition that he may have been the son of the widow of Nain, whom Jesus had earlier brought back to life, and who now in his turn gave his life for the Master.

[1] Simon of Cyrene, Epiphanius xxiv, 3.
[2] Tabari on 4, 156.
[3] Fihrist, p 335, ll. 7 and 8.
[4] Fihrist, p. 336.

CHAPTER V

The Conflict with the Quraish

WE have very little definite information concerning the thirteen years which are supposed to have passed between the time of Mohammed's prophetic call and his flight to Medina. But in compensation for this lack of historical detail we have a much better grasp of the total historical situation. The Koran itself is a source of immeasurable value for the understanding of Mohammed's inner life, of the motives which prompted his message, and of the arguments and objections which his countrymen raised against his preaching. It is quite remarkable that Western scholarship has been so reluctant to exploit adequately the sacred book of Islam as a first-hand source for the inner life of the Prophet, and to treat it as a *document humain,* that enables us to trace a soul which wrestles with its fate, and with naïve candour reveals its aims and hopes, as well as its faults and accomplishments, its weakness and courage.

There are several reasons for this. For Mohammedans the Koran is the most miraculous book in the world. As one theologian states, every prophet is supposed to perform a miracle as a proof of his office. Allah selected this miracle from the particular sphere which happened to be a special object of interest and pride to the contemporaries of the prophet. At the time of Moses the magician was held in high honour. Therefore Allah permitted Moses to perform a miracle with his staff which excelled all of the accomplishments of the Egyptian magicians. In Jesus' day the art of healing occupied the centre of the stage. For this reason Jesus performed wonderful cures, more remarkable than the cures of any other healer. In Mohammed's time the Arabs regarded nothing more highly than the ability to express oneself strikingly, fluently, and with poetic power. Therefore

Allah gave Mohammed the Koran as a miracle which is and will be for all time an unsurpassable model of eloquence. The miraculous quality of the Koran consists in its style, which is such that it unites within itself the five chief types of eloquence, and hence it cannot be imitated either by men or by demons.

But gradually, owing to rationalistic scruples, many began to doubt the pious belief in this miraculous beauty of style. In the golden age of the Caliphate, when the educated classes had acquired a discriminating literary taste, it was realized that the sacred book was not so inimitable as Mohammed believed. Godless literati imitated the style of the book with indisputable cleverness, and liberal theologians dared to assert that the miraculousness of the Koran did not reside in its style, but in the fact that Allah had prevented men from accepting the challenge of the Prophet to write Suras like his own, although as a matter of fact it might have been quite possible for them to do so. The eloquence of the Koran has made even less impression on the Occident. Voltaire called it 'an incomprehensible book which violates our common sense upon every page,' and since Voltaire most European readers have found that the Koran is the most boresome reading that can be imagined.

Certainly this unfavourable estimate is due in no small measure to the form in which the Koran has come down to us. When the scattered revelations were collected into a unified whole at the time of Caliph Uthman the editors applied a very peculiar principle. Without the slightest attention to the actual chronological sequence, they simply placed the longest Suras at the beginning and the shortest at the end, which means that in general the revelations in Medina were placed first, and that the oldest Suras, which are the most interesting in respect of their poetry and their style, were placed at the end. This arrangement makes the understanding of the Koran as a personal document very difficult, and the ordinary reader, who studies the book without technical guidance, cannot understand it at all.

However, although certain passages are characterized by genuine beauty of style, it must be admitted that as a whole the Koran can hardly be regarded as fascinating reading. Yet in itself that does not signify a lack of literary gifts on the part of the author. We must remember that Mohammed never read the Koran, as we do, as one connected whole. He himself could never have had the opportunity of discovering how tiresome the stories of the prophets can be when they are brought together, especially those of the second and third periods in Mecca, with their eternal repetitions. For the Prophet himself these sermons and poems were the beginning of a struggle full of inner tension. But when they are put together they make about the same impression as would be produced if the extemporaneous discourses of a good pulpit orator upon an identical text were read in succession from a collection of sermons. The form does not do justice to their value and originality.

Tradition asserts that during the first three years of his activity in Mecca, the Prophet did not attack the pagan gods. During this interval comparatively good relations are supposed to have existed between him and the Quraish. One of the earliest authorities, Al-Zuhri[1] (d. 713), gives us the following account of the first appearance of the Prophet: 'Secretly and publicly Allah's Apostle called men to Islam, and those who were willing among the young men and the common people accepted the call of Allah, and the number of those who believed the Prophet increased greatly. The unbelievers of the Quraish tribe did not oppose what he said. If he passed the place where they sat together they pointed to him and said: "This young man of the tribe of Abd al-Muttalib proclaims a message from heaven!" This they continued to do until Allah began to attack their gods whom they served beside Him, and until He proclaimed that their fathers who died in unbelief were lost. Then they began to hate the Prophet and show their enmity to him.'

On the whole the Koran substantiates this traditional in-

[1] Baihaki, *Dala'il al-nubuwwa*, cod. Tornberg 232, fol. 83b.

terpretation. At first Mohammed really seems to have been on comparatively good terms with his people. He shared their interests and sympathies. He, who at a later period so often threatened the godless city that Allah would send His punishment upon it, still rejoiced over Mecca's proud national memory of the defeat of the elephant host, without considering that the Abyssinians were Christians, while their conquerors were pagans; and with grateful joy he admonished his people to worship together the Lord of the Ka'ba who protected the peaceful commerce of the city. He endeavoured to remain on good terms with the leading men of the city, and did his utmost to enjoy their good will. Later, when the break had already come, he uttered bitter accusations against himself for having rejected the poor in his zeal to win over the leaders. In Sura 80 Allah makes a serious indictment against the Prophet: 'He frowned, and he turned his back, because the blind man came to him! But what assured thee that he would not be cleansed by the Faith, or be warned, and the warning profit him? As to him who is wealthy—to him thou wast all attention, yet is it not thy concern if he be not cleansed? But as to him who cometh to thee in earnest, and full of fears—him dost thou neglect' (80, 1-10). This is not only an interesting proof of the personal awakening which Mohammed's message brought about among the poor and insignificant inhabitants of Mecca, but it is also an honest and touching criticism of his own arrogant ideas. However, it would make an even better impression upon us if the Prophet had not waited to abandon the attempt to persuade the wealthy until he was seemingly convinced of its futility. The prominent men, on their part, do not appear to have entertained wholly unfriendly feelings toward the young man. According to Sura 11, 65 the unbelievers among the people of Thamud said to their prophet Salih: 'Our hopes were fixed on thee till now; forbiddest thou us to worship what our fathers worshipped?' Mohammed's portrayals of the relations between the men of God of antiquity and the nations to which they were sent are borrowed so completely from his experiences with the Quraish that we have every reason to believe that in this case also he is repeating what he heard concerning his own people. In this earliest period Mohammed advanced the thesis that the three Meccan goddesses were in reality angels to whom one might appeal as advocates before Allah, a thesis which he later rejected, and perhaps even interpreted as a satanic inspiration.

Soon, however, a complete rupture occurred between him and the leaders in Mecca. Step by step we are able to see how the conflict reached a climax, how the accusations of opponents became increasingly bitter, how more and more ruthlessly they poured out their scorn and contempt upon the man who had so deeply wounded their religious and social pride, and how Mohammed himself grew more passionate in attack and defence. It is evident that a catastrophe was inevitable.

What brought this rupture to pass? It has been said that the worldly and unscrupulous merchants of Mecca turned against the new doctrine with such bitter hatred on account of their interest in the profitable commerce which depended upon the pilgrimages, and their fear lest Mohammed's attack upon paganism would abolish the cult of the Ka'ba. They had little interest in the old gods as such, and they themselves hardly believed in anything, but in their worldly wisdom they realized that Mohammed's inherently harmless and naïve fantasies might have fateful consequences for the business life upon which Mecca's prosperity depended.

However, this interpretation of the meaning of the conflict is in direct contrast with the Koran's clear and inescapable description of the situation. And besides, such an interpretation attempts to explain the history of an earlier period from standpoints which are derived from a later period and another realm of culture. In ancient society we cannot presuppose the development of those materialistic economic interests which are characteristic of the industrial captains and financial barons of recent times. To the man of antiquity religion and economics, piety and the desire for profits, had entered into a close combination, in which neither he nor the outsider was able to distinguish the one element from the other. Then, too, such an interpretation is based upon the oft-mentioned but partially incorrect assumption that the old Arabian paganism was at that time in such a state of rapid decay that it had degraded into a meaningless external form which might at any time be abandoned without regret. In popular religion external form is never meaningless. Its power resides, *inter alia*, precisely in the fact that the existing cult form—that is, the rites which were practised by men's ancestors—possess the quality of religious sanctity and belong to the sphere of things holy. The views and opinions of the individual in matters of religion are of less importance. Here there is often a very wide measure of tolerance. Popular religion is not really sensitive until the common cult is involved. Then its most important function seems to be challenged. For this reason it often becomes really intolerant when the mystical and sacred bond which unites the members of the community is in danger of being destroyed by the abandonment of the cult.

Regarded in this light the conflict between Mohammed and his countrymen is, as far as I can see, quite typical. Every sentence of his discussions with his countrymen shows that they clung to the pagan gods and customs with a devout loyalty which possessed an unmistakably religious colouring. The only passage which might be cited in proof of the view that Mohammed's conflict with the Quraish could be interpreted as a conflict with their economic interests is Sura 28, 57: 'But they say, "If we follow the way in which thou art guided, we shall be driven from our country! But have we not established for them a sacred and secure precinct, in which fruits of every kind, our gift for their support, are gathered together?"' The words which speak of the possibility of being driven out of the country by a foreign hostile force—the commentaries mention an alliance of Arabian tribes against Mecca—do not refer to the danger that the acceptance of Mohammed's religion would necessarily involve the economic ruin of the city, owing to the decay of the Ka'ba cult. Also, Mohammed's reply that it is Allah who gives them peace and prosperity would have been a mere wild gesture had his opponents thought that his message was a direct threat to the Ka'ba and the pilgrimage. Mohammed never spoke a word against this cult. According to his opinion, and that of the others also, the Ka'ba was consecrate to Allah, and from the very beginning to the end of the Prophet's career it was the sanctuary of his heart, the holy House of Allah. To be sure, the Bedouin were undoubtedly more conservative in their religion than the city-dwellers. But the danger of being driven out of the country by a hostile attack—and it might have been thought that this would have been called forth as an act of revenge on the part of the local protective gods—would have been primarily a makeshift argument. The Meccans, who were aware of the religious tolerance of Arabia, could feel reasonably safe as to the political developments which might be evoked by Mohammed's belief in a single God, and this argument is never again introduced into the discussion.

However, according to the description in the Koran, the conflict between Mohammed and his people had two aspects which are closely related: a religious and a social aspect. Many of his countrymen responded to the message of the resurrection and the judgment with denial and scorn. 'It is nonsense that we shall come to life again after we have become decayed bones. We never heard such things from our fathers; they are fantasies and old fables.' Although it is a fact that a message of judgment and retribution disturbs and injures the natural sense of security, this part of Mohammed's preaching provoked only contempt and derision. The breach became more serious when the issue was defined between monotheism and the pagan conception of the gods. Mohammed's attack upon the ancient gods aroused attention, so that the people, or rather their leaders, united in determined resistance: 'Maketh he the gods to be but one god? A strange thing forsooth is this! And their chiefs took themselves off. Go, said they, and cleave steadfastly to your gods. Ye see the thing aimed at. We heard not of this in the previous creed. It is but an imposture' (38, 4-6). In this opposition to the proclaiming of the one God who has no equal (*sharik*, actually partner or associate) we sense not only the bitterness which may provoke a frank conflict of interests, but also the deep, instinctive hatred which shows that the attack has struck a blow at men's innermost convictions and a genuine living faith. When in the Koran Mohammed calls upon Allah alone they turn their backs upon him in disgust (17, 49); when Allah alone is worshipped 'the hearts of those who believe not in the life to come are shrivelled up,' but they are filled with joy when the other gods are named (39, 46). As Schwally has pointed out, it is significant that his opponents insisted that the religion of their fathers was being abandoned. Sacred customs are intimately bound up with piety toward men's ancestors, and toward the major traditions of a tribe. Mohammed knew what he was about when he called upon the believers, at the conclusion of the pilgrimage rites, to 'remember Allah as ye remember your own fathers, or with a yet more intense remembrance' (2, 196).

Tribal religion unites the present generation with the past, but it is also the bond which holds living members together. It preserves a balance and proper order, and this, from the conservative standpoint, is the natural and the only possible social pattern. That the custom which has been inherited from men's ancestors should be preserved, that he to whom they are due should enjoy influence and prestige, that the man who belongs once and for all among the lesser and the subordinate should know his place—that is the ideal of conservative authorities, and, in normal circumstances, of the popular religions also. It is for this reason that the innermost and decisive element in the conflict between Mohammed and his people—namely, the social aspect—is so intimately bound up with the religious element.

For the conflict is primarily a matter of prestige. It is primarily the men (*el-mala*, the council) who are the opponents of Mohammed and the other prophets, and they are the wealthiest and most influential citizens, composing the leading circles of the city (7, 64; 11, 29; 23, 24; 38, 5; comp. 23, 33-34). The chief motive of their enmity is arrogance and pride. 'Shall we follow a single man from among ourselves? Then verily should we be in error and in folly. To him alone among us is the office of warning entrusted? No! he is an imposter, an insolent person' (54, 24-25). Further, they say: 'Had but this Koran been sent down to some great one of the two cities!' (43, 30). When the Prophet admonishes them to fall down before the Merciful One, they angrily reply as follows: 'Who is the Merciful? Shall we bow down to what thou biddest?' (25, 61). Like his predecessors among the prophets, Mohammed is told: 'The meanest only are thy followers' (26, 111; 11, 29). The people of Midian say to their prophet Shuaib: 'We understand not much of what thou sayest, and we clearly see that thou art powerless among us. Were it not for thy family we would have surely stoned thee, nor couldst thou have prevailed against us' (11, 93). The opponents continually insinuate that Mohammed's whole bearing is aiming only at the achievement of privilege and power. His real motive is self-exaltation, the desire to play the leading role. He has to defend himself against the accusation of trying to gain something that does not belong to him (38, 86), and he has to insist that he is seeking no reward, neither gold nor power, although he cannot drive away those who believe in him. For he cannot forbid believers to join him.

What aroused the indignation of the leading circles, then, was that a common man, who was not only like all other men, but who possessed no natural claim to authority and prestige, should set himself up as a prophet and claim to have authority over others. If such a thing were to occur at all the claimant would have to be one who had an acknowledged right to leadership. The resentment toward the preeminence which Mohammed attributed to himself, a claim which the wealthy aristocrats in Mecca regarded as an impossible presumption, could not have been due to the revelation, to the religious call as such! They themselves would hardly have aspired to become clairvoyants or poets had they received fantastic revelations from an invisible spirit. What they regarded as a challenge, an attack upon their natural rights, was the claim that the prophetic office involved a certain measure of power and prestige. And as a matter of fact, even in Mecca Mohammed was occupied with the creation of a religio-political society, a state within a state. No matter how tiny the group was, and in spite of the efforts of the opposition to portray it as negligible and unimportant, the Prophet did control a group which was loyally united to him. The disdain which was expressed by those who took pains to call it a handful of miserable nobodies was at the same time a sign of a certain nervousness and wounded pride. His opponents often used every influence within their control to keep the proletariat, the weak and the slaves, from joining the new prophet. We often read how the powerful prevent the weak from following Allah's way (7, 43; 11, 29; 14, 3; 22, 25, etc.). On the Day of Judgment the oppressed and the weak shall say to the haughty rulers: "But for you we had been believers . . . ye bade us believe not in God, and gave Him peers" (34, 30-32).

Thus the religious difference led necessarily to a social conflict, a bitter struggle for power over men, and in this form it developed into a decisive crisis which could only end in annihilation for one and victory for the other party. When this phase of the struggle between Mohammed and the Quraish is kept in mind, it becomes evident that Mohammed's conception of his prophetic position could not have altered so quickly after his emigration to Medina as is frequently supposed. It was really clear to the opposition in Mecca that adherence to his faith signified a certain rejection of national solidarity, and that an acknowledgment of the personal authority of the Prophet involved a break with the existing social authority of that rather informal power of individual leaders which was rooted in custom and tradition. Mohammed did not have to invent the theocratic ideal of a religious society which was at the same time a political group, for this ideal necessarily evolved out of the logic of events, and it seems that his enemies, with the keen penetration of their hatred, saw the inherent necessity of this development before the Prophet himself was aware of it.

Even though we are able to understand, in its essential points, the issue involved in the bitter conflict in Mecca, nevertheless the argument by which his opponents sought to prove the falsity of Mohammed's prophetic claims is still ambiguous at several points. It is quite obvious that in the last phase of the struggle his adversaries in Mecca did not judge these claims as one might have expected in view of their Arabian presuppositions. At first the troublesome preacher was disposed of with the statement: he has a *jinni*, he is a fortune-teller or a poet, an inspired man, like others who were known among the people of Arabia. But later on Mohammed's message was regarded from another and an unexpected point of view. His claim was rejected for the reason that he, who was only a human being, could expect that men should acknowledge him as an ambassador of Allah.

Of course, such objections are partly conditioned by the Prophet's own preaching. It was quite natural that the pagans should want to see the angel to whom Mohammed so often referred, that they should demand that he should finally show them the glorious garden dotted with trees which he had promised as the reward of believers, and that they should crave a sign such as Moses (28, 48) and other men of God showed to their people. These and other ironical objections were directly provoked by Mohammed's preaching. But it is more difficult to understand how the pagans in Mecca could have claimed that Allah ought really to have sent an angel with the revelation (6, 8; 15, 7; 17, 97; 41, 13 etc.), and that an apostle who was a man like all other men, who ate food and frequented the bazaars (25, 8), had no right to demand that men should believe him. Where did the Meccans get this conception that God's ambassador had to be a superhuman and heavenly being? It seems that the opinion of the literate nations concerning Mohammed is reflected here. From the orthodox Jewish or Christian standpoint the thought of any kind of addition or substitution in the sacred canonical writings would seem blasphemous and absurd. Such a thing presupposed an absolute miracle. A new revelation must descend literally from heaven. It is also thought that an echo of Jewish or Christian polemic may be heard in the reviling of the Prophet for receiving the Koran in separate parts, since it ought to have been revealed all at once (15, 91; 25, 34), and preferably written in a book (6, 7) in a foreign tongue (41, 44), like other sacred scriptures.

The stories from the older traditions concerning the sufferings of the Prophet and his followers in Mecca are quite consistent with what is stated in the Koran. The persecution of Mohammed was of a very underhanded nature. As long as he was protected by his uncle and his clan a serious threat to his safety was out of the question. His opponents had to content themselves with plotting against the Prophet in secret meetings (17, 50-51; 21, 3; 23, 69; 43, 79), and with maligning and ridiculing him. Baihaki,[1] in his book *Proof of Prophecy* (a manuscript in the library of the University of Upsala), relates that Amru ibn el Aas was asked, what was the hardest thing which the Prophet was obliged to suffer from the Quraish? He answered: 'I was once present when the chief among the idolaters assembled at the Ka'ba. They were discussing Allah's Apostle, and said: "Never have we had to tolerate from anyone what we have had to tolerate from this man. He slanders our fathers, criticizes our religion, divides our people, and blasphemes our gods. Such grievous things have we tolerated from this man, etc." Meanwhile the Apostle of Allah approached. He touched the corner of the Ka'ba and passed by those assembled in order to walk around

[1] Baihaki, *Dala'il al-ncbuwwa*, coc. Tornberg 232, fol. 85a.

the sanctuary. They heaped abuse upon him as he passed. and it was evident that he understood what they were saying. This was repeated three times. The third time he stopped and said: "Men of Quraish! I will surely repay you for this with interest!" His words so affected the men that there was not one among them who did not sit as still as if he were carrying a bird upon his head. Finally, in order to pacify him, the man who had formerly been the worst of the group said: "Go, Abu-l-Kasim, you are no fool." During the night his enemies regretted their caution. The next day, when they again met Mohammed at the Ka'ba, they all rushed toward him and surrounded him, and said: "Are you he who abuses our gods and our religion?" He replied: "Yes, it is I who speak thus." Then I saw that a man seized his cloak. Abu Bekr now arose and said, with tears: "Woe to you, will you kill a man because he says, Allah is my Lord?" Then they went away. This was the hardest thing that he was compelled to suffer at their hands.' Another time his worst enemy, his uncle Abu Jahl, and several of his companions, took the uterus of a newly slaughtered camel and struck the Prophet between the shoulders with it as he was bowed in prayer. Then Mohammed spoke three times: 'Allah! Thou must repay the Quraish for this!' Therewith he mentioned by name seven of his bitterest enemies. All seven of them died as unbelievers at Bedr. The story states that this was the only time that the Prophet was heard to petition Allah for the punishment of enemies.

The external sufferings which the Prophet was compelled to undergo were apparently not very severe. Matters were serious for those of his followers who were socially weak and unprivileged, the poor strangers and slaves. According to tradition the negro slave Bilal, who is said to have been the first muezzin, and other believers, were clothed in iron mail-shirts and put in the burning heat of the sun, and they were tortured in other ways. The old slave-woman Sumayya, whom Abu Jahl killed with a lance, is supposed to be the first martyr of Islam.

But the persecution of the faithful could hardly have been so terrible as this. Certainly Mohammed would not have refrained from mentioning and condemning such outrageous attacks. Nevertheless, that the position of the believers in Mecca was miserable is shown by the circumstance that Mohammed permitted part of his followers to migrate to Abyssinia. This shows a significant change in Mohammed's political views. Previously he had derided the Abyssinians because of their unsuccessful attack upon the Ka'ba. Now the enemies of his countrymen had become his natural friends. It also shows that Mohammed felt that Christianity was most closely related to his own belief. And the Christians, on their part, seemed to show sympathy and understanding for the new message. Of all men, he says, the Jews and idolaters are most hostile to the true believers. But 'thou shalt certainly find those to be nearest in affection to thee who say, "We are Christians." This, because some of them are priests and monks, and because they are free from pride. And when they hear that which hath been sent down to the Apostle, thou seest their eyes overflow with tears at the truth they recognize therein, saying, "O our Lord! we believe!" ' (5, 85-86).

However, Mohammed's preaching did not fall only upon unbelieving hearts. A not inconsiderable group gradually flocked together to receive the new revelation. From tradition, and still more from the Koran, it can be seen that the majority of these believers came from among the poor and insignificant, who were naturally more receptive to the gospel of judgment and Paradise. To a gifted man who felt called to accomplish great things this fact must naturally have caused disappointment. With his strong realistic sense Mohammed must often have told himself that the conversion of a single outstanding individual would mean more for the success of his cause than the winning of a dozen poor unfortunates. With an integrity which deserves to be recognized he allows Allah to admonish His prophet not to despise these insignificant men, but to show mercy to them, and not to reject them:

'Let not thine eyes be turned away from them in quest of the pomp of this life' (18, 27; 6, 52; 26, 215).

Some among those who joined themselves to Mohammed in this early period, when the profession of Islam was nothing more than a stumbling-block to the Jews, and foolishness to the pagans, were many important and gifted personalities, men of moral earnestness, with a healthy sense of reality. The chapter dealing with these co-labourers and friends is not the least important in the biography of the Prophet. What his own actions and words only partially disclose: the force of his personality, the trust which he engendered, the enthusiasm which he awakened, and the uprightness which characterized his inmost nature, is all engraved here in living letters. It will suffice to mention his two most outstanding friends, his immediate successors as leaders of the congregation of Islam, Abu Bekr and Umar. Abu Bekr had been an intimate friend of Mohammed even before the Prophet received his prophetic call, and he became one of his first followers. With unwavering loyalty, and with a faith which seemed to be free from all hesitation and doubt, he followed him on his journey from humiliation to power. Mohammed is said to have claimed that if the faith of all men were weighed against the faith of Abu Bekr, his faith would outweigh them all. He had already sacrificed the greater part of his possessions for the Prophet's cause when he accompanied him on the flight to Medina, and what he regained later was given for the equipment of the formidable campaign against Syria. On this occasion Umar thought that he would surpass Abu Bekr. When Umar came with his gift and the Prophet asked him what he had reserved for the support of his family, he answered: 'Only half of my possessions.' But when the same question was asked of Abu Bekr he answered: 'Allah.' He had given all that he possessed. Abu Bekr was known by the name As-Siddiq, 'the upright,' and all that we know of his faultless character shows that he was entitled to this name.

The second Caliph of Islam unquestionably deserves a place

of honour among the most famous of the rulers of history. Many have borne the appellation 'the great,' but with much less justification than Umar. In the earliest history of Islam he is one of the best representatives of the new religious ideal, a true believer without blemish, a man of sincerity and power, with hard hands but with an upright heart. During the period of his rule over the mightiest empire in the world he lived in the same Spartan simplicity that he had known in the years of privation in Medina. Some of the companions of the Prophet who were deemed especially pious, and who were counted among the ten to whom Paradise had already been promised here upon earth, accumulated gigantic fortunes in the course of the wars of conquest. One of them, Zubeir, left fifty million dirhems; Umar, on the other hand, used only two dirhems per diem of the State revenue for his own needs.[1] He held that the ruler must manage the revenue of the treasury as a guardian should manage property entrusted to him. It was a striking scene when the Caliph apportioned the spoils among the believers, giving something to each, with the exception of his own son. This son sat there the whole time, as still as a lamb with a broken leg, although he alone received nothing from his father. In private life Umar practised an ascetic simplicity. He rode upon a donkey with a saddle made of bast, and wore a coat and shoes which he had mended with his own hands. He went about the streets and the bazaars with a riding-switch in his hand and pronounced legal judgments, without formality, while standing upon his feet.

A puritanical earnestness characterized his nature. Song and jest were silenced when his large energetic figure appeared. It is told that the Prophet himself, who was usually not fond of poetry, but who could tolerate it when it glorified Islam and ridiculed his enemies, was once listening to the recitation of a poet. But when Umar approached the Prophet commanded the poet to be silent, and explained: 'Umar

[1] Ibn Abd Rabbihi, *Al-iqd al-farid*, Cairo, 1305, i, p. 201.

dislikes such vanity.'[1] Once he came to the Prophet when several cousins and aunts were visiting him. The women were carrying on a loud conversation, in spite of the exalted presence of the Prophet. But when Umar entered they retreated in fear behind the curtain. When Umar then angrily inquired whether it were not more fitting to show respect to the Prophet than to himself, they answered: 'We are afraid of you because you are strict and harsh.' Then the Prophet said: 'By Him who hath my soul in His hands! If the devil himself were to meet you on the street he would dodge into a side-alley!'[2] And in fact Islamic legend[3] does tell how the mighty Umar brought fear into the heart of the Devil himself. According to the legend the Devil came to the Prophet one day, and asked: 'Is it possible for me to repent?' And Allah's Apostle answered: 'Yes, go to Adam's grave, prostrate yourself and kiss the earth, and then Allah may forgive you.' (It should be remembered that according to the Koran Satan's fall was due to his refusal to prostrate himself before Adam.) Joyfully the Devil set out to find Adam's grave. But on the way he met Umar, who asked him 'Where are you going, and what are you up to?' The Devil stated his purpose. Then Umar said: 'Allah can never forgive you. When He commanded you to bow down before Adam, while he yet lived, you refused, but now when the Prophet commands you to kiss the ground upon Adam's grave you are willing to obey. Shame on you, you miserable wretch!' The spiteful polemic of the Shiites uses this legend as a reason for asserting that the Devil has corrupted all men, but Umar has corrupted the Devil. For had it not been for the fierce Umar, the Devil himself might have been converted.

With unrelenting sternness Umar enforced the sacred commandments of the Koran and the regulations of the Prophet. When his own son committed the offence of drinking wine

[1] Sharaf Ali bin al-Wali, *Rijad al-Jinan*, Bombay, 1312, p. 342.
[2] Bukhari, *Kitab bad' al-Khalq, bab manaqib al-muhajirin.*
[3] Sharaf Ali, p. 342.

he punished him so severely that the son collapsed afterward and cried out: 'You have killed me!' Umar replied: 'Then go and tell Allah how your father enforces his punishments.'[1]

In spite of his gruffness the great Caliph was by no means self-contained and unapproachable. He dealt with his subordinates with patriarchal simplicity, and gladly accepted advice, 'even from a woman.' Insignificant and needy people often found that the dreaded ruler could be kind and helpful. He frequently travelled incognito in order to ascertain the circumstances in which his subjects lived. In the course of his journey home from Jerusalem he came unrecognized to an old woman who complained bitterly that Umar had not given her a penny of the spoils. 'How should Umar know how you are faring?' asked the stranger. She replied: 'Do you think that he who has been made ruler of the nation should not know how his country is faring?' Then Umar exclaimed: 'Poor Umar! an old woman knows what is right better than you!' Then he paid the claim of 25 dinars which the old woman thought she had upon the Commander of the Faithful, and had a deed inscribed upon parchment. When he returned home he gave it to his son, saying: 'Place this paper in my hand when I am dead so that I may show it to Allah when I stand before His throne.'[2]

So the legends delighted in describing the great Caliph. He was a child of the people and a man of the people, of whom it is said that 'his riding-whip was feared more than the sword of the tyrants: his conversion was the victory of Islam and his government an act of God's mercy toward his people.'

During the most difficult period in Mecca, when the position of the Prophet seemed completely hopeless, Umar had unexpectedly joined his company. A man of his strong, independent will must often have found it hard to bow to the will of another, and there were times when his straight-

[1] Damiri, *Kitab al-hayawan*, Cairo, 1330, i, p. 620.
[2] Damiri, *Kitab al-hayawan*, Cairo, 1330, i, p. 88.

forward, upright nature rebelled against Mohammed's opportunistic policy, which impressed him as being a denial of the principles of Islam. Yet he always bowed to the superior personality, and ultimately realized what unconquerable and consistent will-power lay concealed behind such apparent yielding.

The actions which seem to cast a shadow upon Mohammed's character are often difficult to interpret, and we are always uncertain whether we have understood and evaluated them correctly. Umar's character reveals no dark areas. He stands before us clear, upright, and without blemish. That such a friend became and remained Mohammed's most loyal helper, in spite of occasional differences of opinion, that the faith and conduct of the Prophet became his *Sunna*, his holy custom, which he maintained and guarded with unalterable consistency, is the most important and conclusive proof of Mohammed's religious and personal integrity.

CHAPTER VI

The Ruler in Medina

MOHAMMED'S Hegira, his flight to Medina, was the turning-point in his career and in the history of Islam. It occurred on the 12th of the month of Rabi'al-awwal, A.D. 622 For a long time he had realized that his work in his native city was all in vain, and so he had long been seeking to make an alliance with the Arabian chiefs who came to Mecca for the great pilgrimage. This shows the falsity of the prevailing idea, that Mohammed appeared in Mecca only as a pious messenger, with a purely religious programme, and without any associated political and social aims, and that it was entirely owing to the fact that circumstances in Medina delivered the political power into his hands that he suddenly assumed the role of a theocratic ruler and laid claim to political authority. As a matter of fact, Mohammed could hardly conceive of a religious community which was not both a social and a political organism. Even in the Meccan period he frequently employed the term *'umma,'* which really signifies 'people' or 'nation,' to describe the brotherhoods which the various prophets had gathered together. A prophet came to each *'umma'* or nation but the followers of each prophet also constituted an *'umma,'* a kind of political entity.

However, the Prophet's attempts to conclude an alliance were unsuccessful until 620, when he met a group of six men from Yathrib at the pilgrim festival at 'Akaba, on the road between 'Arafat and Mina. They listened willingly to his preaching and his recitation of the Koran. According to Ibn Ishak's story, this was because there were many Jews in their native city, who had told them once, when they were fighting with the Arabs, that a prophet would soon appear to help them conquer the pagans. These six men from Yathrib took Mohammed to be this prophet, and were eager to get ahead of the Jews by recognizing him. Thus the legend has it. Of course, the people of Medina could not have regarded Mohammed as a Jewish prophet. But it is possible that in some way the many Jews in Medina did prepare the way for Islam. Monotheism, the resurrection, and belief in a written Divine revelation were certainly more familiar in Medina than in Mecca. But the internal conditions within the city constitute the primary reason why the men of Medina fixed their attention upon Mohammed. In contrast with Mecca, which was dominated by one tribe, the Quraish, Medina was divided into two Arab tribes, the Aus and the Khazraj, and three Jewish tribes, Banu Nadir, Banu Kainuka, and Banu Karaiza. A destructive feud had long been raging between the two Arab tribes, a state of general uncertainty prevailed, and the absence of a unified authority destroyed the hope of more favourable conditions.

Although Mohammed was at a disadvantage as against the rich and powerful merchants of Mecca, he continued to exercise some authority, and he had a number of followers who could not be ignored. In Medina he might become the deciding factor in the civil strife.

The six men spread the news about Mohammed in Yathrib, and the following year, at 'Akaba, he met twelve men from Medina who entered into a formal agreement with him. They agreed to eschew idolatry, theft, and adultery, to refrain from killing their infant daughters, to tell no lies, and to obey Mohammed in all good things. When they returned to their native city Mohammed sent with them a reader who could teach them the Koran and instruct them in Islam. This first missionary of Islam met with such success that at the next pilgrimage seventy-three men and two women came from Yathrib to join with the Prophet in Mecca. Then the formal protective agreement was renewed at 'Akaba. The men of Medina promised to defend the Prophet as they would protect their own wives and children, and if necessary to fight for his sake against the blacks and the reds—that is, against Negroes and Arabs. The contract was confirmed by Mohammed shaking hands with twelve especially selected men.

Mohammed's followers then began to migrate from Mecca to Medina, until finally only the Prophet, Abu Bekr, and Ali remained in the city. When 'Hegira' is translated by the term 'flight' this is of course linguistically incorrect, but in substance it is justified. Mohammed's emigration was a flight. Islamic tradition points out that it was the intention of the unbelievers to kill the Prophet after he was cut off from the protection of his tribal kinsmen. However, their purpose seemed to be rather that of keeping him in the city. Presumably they knew his plans, and realized that he might become a dangerous enemy as the leader in Medina.

So Mohammed, accompanied by Abu Bekr, secretly departed from his native city and proceeded to a cave in Jebel Thaur, where they remained hidden while the Quraish searched for them. The pious legends tell how Allah marvellously watched over His Apostle. When the persecutors came to the cave they observed that a pair of doves had built their nest at the entrance, and so they concluded that the cave was empty. Mohammed himself speaks of the wonderful peace, and the sense of the presence of God, which filled his soul in these fateful hours of his life (9, 40). After three days Mohammed left the cave and arrived safely in Medina.

Here his first concern was to build a mosque (Arabic *masjid*, place of prayer). With the co-operation of all of his followers, who were later divided into 'emigrants' from Mecca and 'helpers' from Medina, he built a simple structure of sun-dried bricks, in which religious services were conducted. Mohammed was no less concerned with strengthening internally the motley crowd which at this time composed his congregation. The principles which he followed are stated in an important document, reproduced in Ibn Ishak's biography,[1] which probably dates from the second year after the Hegira, and is a congregational constitution for Medina.

[1] Ibn Hisham, i, p. 278.

In this document it is stated that the believers of the tribe of Quraish, and those from Yathrib, as well as those who follow them, join with them, and fight with them, shall constitute 'one congregation, one *umma*, separate from other men.' However, within this unity the emigrants are to form one group and their helpers another, in so far as each group must demand and pay penalties for itself, and buy the freedom of its own slaves. If one believer rebels against the others, and stirs up strife, enmity, and insurrection, the whole congregation must turn against him, regardless of the group to which he belongs. A believer may not kill a fellow-believer for the sake of an unbeliever, nor may he support an unbeliever against a believer. Disagreements arising in the congregation are to be brought before Allah and His Apostle. Here we meet for the first time this formula, so significant for Mohammed's growing self-consciousness. It shows us that the Prophet, with increasing assurance, has come to regard his judicial decisions as the verdicts of Allah Himself.

The laws of the Medina congregation are the first draft of the theocratic constitution which gradually made Islam a world empire and a world religion. In the community of believers the old tribal constitution was abrogated in all essentials. Whosoever acts contrary to the religious authority cannot even be protected by his nearest relatives. Islam is to become not only a religion but also a brotherhood. 'Only the faithful are brethren,' Sura 49, 10 declares. Allah has indeed divided men into various peoples and tribes, but He did that only so they could distinguish each other (49, 13), and not so that these distinctions should constitute an insuperable barrier to religious unity.

In order to tighten still more the bond between the emigrants and their helpers, Mohammed caused each one of his followers from Mecca to enter a personal and fraternal bond with some Medina disciple. At first he tried to win the Jews by making concessions to their religious customs. For example, in conformity with the Jewish custom, he commanded believers to turn their faces toward Jerusalem when praying, and he adopted *'Ashura*, the great day of atonement of the Jews, which at this time fell upon the tenth of the month of Muharram, as a festival.

Even though the Prophet succeeded beyond all expectation in welding the believers into a unified and devoted organization, and soon even into a valiant and self-sacrificing army, nevertheless his attempt to win the Jews proved fruitless. The Jews of Medina soon formed their own conclusions about Mohammed. They noticed that in most things he deviated from Jewish ideas and customs, and in particular that his knowledge of the sacred scriptures was extremely deficient. They mercilessly exposed his misunderstandings and distortions, and revealed his weaknesses with bitter scorn. The revelations which date from the first period in Medina aim at counteracting the attacks of the Jews, which threatened completely to destroy Mohammed's religious authority. The arguments which Mohammed employed in his polemic were largely borrowed from Christianity.[1] When the Jews disputed his claim that the Arabian Prophet is mentioned in their sacred scriptures, he replied that their scriptures were corrupted. The Christian theologians had already made this old accusation against the Jews to account for the deviations of the Greek translation from the Hebrew text. Following the example of the Christian theologians, he too interpreted the laws of sacrifice and purification as a special punishment which God had imposed upon the Jews because of their rebelliousness. When the enmity of the Jews developed Mohammed withdrew the concession which he had previously made to the Jewish rites. For a while he seemed to be in doubt concerning the direction in which believers should face when they pray. Finally the decision was reached: 'We have seen thee turning thy face toward every part of Heaven; but we will have thee turn to a *qibla* which shall please thee. Turn then thy face towards the sacred Mosque' (2, 139).

So the sanctuary in Mecca became for all time the point

[1] Andrae, *Ursprung des Islams*, K.H.A., 1925, pp. 104 ff.

toward which believers turn in prayer. In his treatise on the pilgrimage festival the eminent Dutch student of Islam, Snouck Hurgronje, has shown what great signifiance this decision of Mohammed's came to have for the whole development of Islam. In Snouck Hurgronje's opinion this change of direction, which made the Ka'ba the sacred spot of Islam, and which was at the same time substantiated by an earlier revelation, is the most brilliant of Mohammed's religious achievements, since the sanctuary in the sacred precinct of Mecca is thereby brought into connection with Abraham.

It must be conceded that Mohammed did here exhibit an ability to straighten out a difficult situation which is by no means restricted to this one case, and that the doctrine of the Ka'ba and the religion of Abraham is tantamount to Islam's declaration of independence, inasmuch as by it the Prophet finally established his emancipation from the cultured peoples. But the roots of this new orientation are really much deeper. From the beginning the temple of his native city was for him the House of Allah. Allah is the Lord of the Ka'ba. It is easy to understand how his reverence for that sanctuary, which was for him the revelation of the holiness of the invisible world, should increase with distance. For at that time migration from home was much more than a spatial change.

Then, too, from the very beginning Mohammed had been happy in the belief that his revelation, the Koran, was in complete agreement with the sacred books of the Jews and Christians. The bitter opposition of the Jews in Medina convinced him that this was not the case. In principle, of course, he did not surrender his own doctrine of revelation, but he lost the practical support for it upon which he had previously depended. In all belief in God there is an element of conservatism. Even when a religion breaks new trails it feels the need of portraying the new message as something which has existed from the very beginning, as something which is tried and true. Eternal validity must somehow be expressed in terms of time. Jesus came to fulfil the law and the prophets. Luther sought only to restore the Gospel and Paul to their rightful place. The God-revealers and prophets of Hellenism always appeal to ancient scriptures, or to the men of God of dim antiquity: Orpheus, Hermes, Moses.

There are several reasons why Mohammed went back specifically to Abraham. Although he was neither a Jew nor a Christian, Abraham was a man of God who was revered and recognized by both Jew and Christian. Mohammed knew that he had lived before the revelation of the Law and the Gospel. But above all, he was the tribal father not only of the Jews, but of the Arabs also, and was therefore especially qualified to be a symbol of the new Arabian religion. Even during the later period in Mecca Mohammed acknowledged him as the tribal father of the Arabs, and probably also associated him with the sanctuary in Mecca (14, 38-40). Through the doctrine of the religion of Abraham the true, pure *Hanif* religion which lies at the back of the scriptural religions, but was falsified by their adherents, and which was now being proclaimed in its original purity by Mohammed, he achieved an authority for his revelation which the attacks of the cultured peoples could not destroy. He had overcome a difficulty which had apparently tormented him more than all that he was forced to endure at the hands of his pagan countrymen in Mecca.

In this way Mohammed solved the political and religious problems created by the migration and the new situation in Medina. But before this another difficulty had appeared, which was less complex, and yet was hardly less difficult of solution. This was the practical question of how the emigrants were to subsist. Medina was a city of gardens. The cultivated land between the two Harras was exploited to the utmost. Here, then, it was hardly possible to make a living by productive labour. And at first the newcomers lived in great poverty, and had to perform hard labour to earn their keep. Ali, the son-in-law of the Prophet, carried water for brickmaking, and received a date for each bucketful. So he earned sixteen dates, and shared this frugal meal with the Prophet, who had nothing. Such stories, of course, should be regarded primarily as products of a pious romanticism which loved to dwell upon the sufferings and privations to which the revered saints were subjected in this early period. But their situation was certainly difficult, and a solution had to be found. It is somewhat disappointing to one who is eager to do justice to Mohammed as an ethical and religious personality to find that he seems almost immediately to surrender to the idea of supporting himself by the occupation which even to-day is the natural source of income for so many Bedouin; namely, banditry. In addition to the fact that in Arabia banditry has always been reckoned more or less explicitly among the permissible occupations and sources of income, it might be said in his defence that his expulsion from his native city made the idea of revenge seem natural and obvious. The people of Mecca had persecuted him to the limit and had rejected Allah's revelation. Any harm that he might do to them was only a just execution of the judgment which the Prophet had prophesied in the name of Allah.

The method, then, which the Prophet employed in order to provide sustenance for himself and all his companions, was that of plundering the caravans which passed Medina on the way to or from Syria. The first weak attempt seems to have ended in failure. The first successful expedition was undertaken in the second year after the Hegira. It is noteworthy, not only because it was on this expedition that the first blood was shed for Islam, but also because it seems to throw a very unfavourable light upon the character of the Prophet. In the month of Rajab—that is, in a month which the Arabs regarded as holy, and during which a general truce prevailed—Mohammed sent out Abdallah Ibn Jahsh with eight men. He gave him a letter and an oral command to travel for two days. Then he was to open the letter and execute the orders which it contained. However, he was not to coerce any of his companions, but must allow each of them to decide whether or not he desired to take part in the proposed expedition. The original wording of this important letter seems to be preserved by Wakidi.[1] 'Go to the valley of Nakhla,' it reads, 'and set an ambush for the Quraish.' Even the earliest tradition felt that this was wrong. This is shown by the fact that the text of the ominous letter has been subjected to various emendations. According to Ibn Ishak it reads: 'Go to Nakhla between Mecca and Taif and there spy on the Quraish in order to bring us news concerning them.' The attempt is thus made to interpret it as though Mohammed originally commanded the expedition only to spy out the intentions of the Quraish. This shows clearly that, like ourselves, the historians of Islam feel the difficulty of completely defending the action of the Prophet in this case. The fact that he commanded Abdallah not to force any of his companions shows us that the plan must also have conflicted with Arabian standards. Ordinarily the Prophet regarded it as the unswerving duty of every true believer to risk life and limb in the cause of Islam.

Apparently Mohammed knew that Abdallah was a man who would understand a hint. When Abdallah read the letter, after the two days had elapsed, he said: 'Those of you who yearn for the martyr's crown, follow me when I proceed to carry out the command of Allah's Apostle. Whoever has no such yearning is permitted to return.' After such a challenge no one could refuse. At the next resting-place, however, two of the companions lost their camels and had to search for them. Thus they found a way of withdrawing from the affair. When they reached the valley of Nakhla, Abdallah and his men soon found the caravan, laden with raisins, leather, and other articles of trade, and guarded by only four men. It is supposed to have been the last day of the month of Rajab, and the six men held a council, and decided that should they postpone the attack the caravan would reach the protected area of Mecca before the end of the month. So they made the attack, killed one man, and captured the caravan.

[1] Wakidi, p. 35.

When Abdallah and his companions returned to Medina, their action aroused great excitement. Their countrymen sternly reprimanded them. The Jews made scornful puns on the name of the murdered man and the participants. And in Mecca it was said that Mohammed had openly broken the truce of the sacred month. But the worst of all was that the Prophet absolutely repudiated his action, and declared that he had in no sense commanded them to fight during the sacred month. At first he let the captured booty remain untouched, and refused to accept the fifth which should have been his share. But after a time, when feeling had subsided, and the loot began to stimulate natural interest, a Koranic revelation concerning it was finally delivered. In Medina the Koran begins to constitute a sort of running commentary on current events, from political incidents and the attacks of opponents to little stories of scandal within the family circle of the Prophet. The revelation which applies here is Sura 2, 214, where Allah declares: 'They will ask thee concerning war in the sacred month. Say: "To war therein is bad, but to turn aside from the cause of Allah, and to have no faith in Him, and the sacred temple, and to drive out its people, is worse in the sight of Allah."' A brilliant example of Mohammed's art of formulation! He has not denied the sanctity of the the month of truce, which is an undeniable demand of Arabian morality, but he has found a way of overlooking Abdallah's act. For he cautiously suggests that in a struggle with such people as the Quraish all methods are permissible. The theologians of Islam have been morally refined enough to feel that this style of speech smacks of Jesuitism, and accordingly they have considered it necessary to ward off, apologetically, the silent objections of which a healthy sense of justice be conscious. 'Allah judges His friends and enemies with equity and justice,' declares Ibn Qayyim al-Jauziyya;[1] 'He does not acquit His friends—but He declares that the sin of His enemies is more grievous and deserves greater condemnation and punishment.

[1] Ibn Qayyim al-Jauziyya, *Zad al-ma'ad*, 1, p. 341.

And above all He asserts that His friends have acted well, even though with a wrong purpose. Therefore Allah forgives them for the sake of their faith and obedience, and because they emigrated with Allah's Apostle, and chose the things of Allah in preference to the world. For it is said: "If the beloved commits a single sin, his many good qualities become a thousand intercessors." '

But even if we consider the difficult situation with which Mohammed was apparently confronted, it can hardly be denied that these events cast a shadow upon his character. It is of course possible that when he dispatched Abdallah's expedition, Mohammed thought only of a possibility that the caravan might not reach the protected area before the end of the month. But the records concerned make this explanation seem hardly plausible. We receive the impression that the Prophet intended the very thing which came to pass. What arouses our criticism is not the circumstance that he broke the truce of the sacred month. I have already emphasized the fact that his views are in general characterized by an emancipation from all ritualistic fussiness and conformity, a tendency to permit common sense to decide in conflicts between the demands of the law and reality. What offends us is the calculating slyness with which he cleverly provokes Abdallah's action without assuming any responsibility for what occurred. This event reveals a trait of his character which is particularly uncongenial to the ideals of manliness of the Nordic races. He lacks the courage to defend an opinion openly, revealing a certain tendency to dodge and take advantage of subterfuges, to avoid an open espousal of his position.

However, the excitement about the Nakhla expedition soon subsided in the face of an event which, although of slight importance in itself, was of crucial significance to Mohammed, and became a bulwark of faith to him, as did the passage of the Red Sea to the Israelites. Six weeks had barely passed since Abdallah's return when Mohammed learned through his spies that a large caravan was approaching on the way home from Syria. It comprised no less than a thousand camels, and most of the merchants of Mecca were involved in the venture, under the leadership of Abu Sufian, the most prominent man in Mecca, and the progenitor of the ruling family of the Umayyads. Mohammed advanced immediately with 305 men and 70 camels, which probably represented the whole extent of the resources which he possessed at that time. The clever Abu Sufian, who had ridden ahead for scouting purposes, became suspicious, and caused the caravan to make a detour towards the sea. In Mecca also Mohammed's plans had become known, and an army of 950 men, 700 camels, and 100 horses was organized. The Quraish started out in jubilant arrogance. The men hurled their spears into the air in order to exhibit their high spirits and their confidence of victory. Three female singers followed the army, and at every camping-place they sang songs to the rhythm of tambourines, kindling the courage of the warriors. When Mohammed discovered that the Quraish were advancing against him he held a council of war to ascertain the feelings of the men of Medina, who were under no obligation to fight outside their own city. Their loyalty stood the test. On the evening of the 17th of Ramadan, in the year 2, the armies met in the Wadi Bedr, 11 miles to the south-west of Medina. The forces were very close to each other, and were prevented from seeing each other only by a sand-hill which separated them. During the night a heavy rain fell, but nevertheless the believers slept soundly. Mohammed afterwards regarded this as a special proof of the manner in which Allah cares for His people. In the morning the forces clashed. Mohammed himself did not take part in the battle. He had spent the night in a shelter of branches which had been erected for him, and after mustering and disposing his men for battle, he repaired to the shelter for prayer. But he had instructed the men how to conduct themselves in battle. They were to fight in closed ranks, bombarding the enemy with arrows, and using their swords only at the last moment. In contrast with his opponents, who fought with careless bravado, without order or plan, and avoiding a real pitched battle, but rather seeking to confine the conflict to a series of hand-to-hand struggles, Mohammed championed a comparatively modern tactical ideal. To the exuberant martial mood and the knightly bravery of the Meccans he opposed strict discipline and careful deliberation. Wakidi tells that the Quraish were seized with terror when they saw the serious and determined faces of the believers. For the emigrants and their brothers war was not a knightly sport or a festive parade to gain national honour. It was as serious as death. Already in this battle we gain an impression of the spirit which dominated the young militant congregation of Islam.

As was customary, the battle began with single combats fought before the hostile forces drawn up in battle array. Ali, Hamza, the uncle of the Prophet, and Ubaida stepped forth in the name of the Moslems, and each of them succeeded in felling his opponent. Like our Nordic forefathers, the Bedouin took an extraordinary interest in descriptions of battle. *Ayyam el-'arab*, 'the Bedouin days of battle' were a welcome theme of poetry and story, and hence such descriptions belong to the material which tradition has preserved with special detail and fidelity. In Wakidi's writings the stories of the battle of Bedr almost fill a small volume. The Quraish were led by Mohammed's mortal enemy, Abu Jahl. The battle waxed hot around him, but his tribesmen surrounded him like an invulnerable fortress. However, Mu'adh Ibn Amr succeeded in breaking through and cutting off Abu Jahl's foot with his sword. His son 'Iqrima retaliated with a blow which severed Mu'adh's arm from the shoulder, so that it hung only by the skin. Mu'adh stepped upon the arm and tore it from his shoulder. Then another Moslem came and dealt Abu Jahl the death-blow.

It was not the human hosts alone who fought at Bedr. As the Nordic warriors heard the steeds of the Valkyries snorting amidst the clamour of battle, and as David in the valley of Rephaim heard footsteps in the tree-tops, where Yahweh advanced to fight against the Philistines, so Gabriel and his hosts fought on the side of the believers at Bedr. A man who saw the battle from a distance, and kept himself behind the ranks of the Moslems, in order to be on hand to plunder the wounded, saw a cloud approaching and heard the snorting of the horses, the clash of weapons, and encouraging battle-cries coming from the cloud. The cloud descended at the place where the forces of the believers were engaged, and now their number, which previously seemed small in contrast with the pagans, appeared to be twice as great. Some said that the angels had fought on the side of the Moslems in the guise of friendly warriors. Others told how the angels wore green, yellow, and red turbans made of light, and how the heads of their horses were decked with white flocks of wool. According to others they fought invisibly. It was observed that hands were cut off and great wounds inflicted, though none saw weapons moving or blood flowing. Finally Mohammed took a handful of sand, pronounced an incantation, and threw the sand at the enemy. Then their army scattered in terror.

By noon the battle was won. The Quraish fled. Forty-nine of the enemy had fallen—Ali had killed twenty-two, either alone, or with the help of others. An equal number were captured. The believers had lost fourteen men on the field of battle. Hard-hearted Umar wanted to kill off the captives, but Mohammed decreed that the Quraish should pay a ransom for them. Among the prisoners was the Prophet's own son-in-law, Abu-l-Aas, who was married to his daughter Zainab. Thus Islam had shattered all ties of kinship. But when, as a ransom for her husband, Zainab sent a golden necklace which had belonged to Khadijah, given to the daughter as a wedding present, Mohammed was touched, and released Abu-l-Aas without a ransom.

Seldom has such an insignificant conflict had such far-reaching consequences. The moral effect, especially in Medina, can hardly be overestimated. The Prophet had received undeniable proof that God was on his side. In Sura 8 he draws the religious conclusion from the victory at Bedr, 'the day of decision,' as he terms it. He reminds the believers how God supported him, how He kept His promise to send angels to help them, how He had bestowed deep sleep and refreshing rain upon them. It was Allah Himself who fought and won the victory: 'So it was not ye who slew them, but God slew them; and those shafts were God's, not thine!' (8, 17). The satisfaction and joy of victory increased the Prophet's consciousness of his calling. The thought grew in him that the world must be compelled by force to obey Allah's words and commandments, if preaching did not succeed: 'Fight then against them till strife be at an end, and the religion shall be wholly God's' (8, 40). Thus, even at this time, shortly after the battle of Bedr, the principle is formulated which for a season made the sword the principal missionary instrument of Islam. Then Mohammed thought only of Arabia. His horizon reached no farther. But the principle was elastic, and it could be extended so long as success expanded the vision of the Prophet. For him who has God on his side nothing is impossible: 'O prophet! stir up the faithful to the fight. Twenty of you who stand firm shall vanquish two hundred, and if there be a hundred of you they shall vanquish a thousand of the infidels' (8, 66). Touchingly the Prophet's pride in his faithful companions emerges: 'He it is who hath strengthened thee with His help, and with the faithful, and hath made their hearts one. Hadst thou spent all the riches of the earth, thou couldst not have united their hearts' (8, 64).

Mohammed used the increased power which he had gained in Medina to take revenge upon his enemies, the Jews. He did not have to wait long for an excuse to attack them. A Jew of the tribe Banu Kainuka played an indecent prank on a married Arab woman. As she was sitting at the marketplace he fastened the skirt of her dress upon her shoulder with a thorn. A Moslem killed the daring jester, and the Jews retaliated by killing the murderer. Mohammed locked up the guilty tribe in its own quarters. After a period of siege they were forced to surrender, on the condition that all their possessions should pass into Mohammed's hands. They themselves were released and removed to Syria. Their property provided a new opportunity for remedying the poverty of the emigrants.

One individual Jew, who had especially aroused Mohammed's bitter hatred, now also fell a victim of his vengeance. This was the poet Ka'b Ibn Al-Ashraf, who, after the battle of Bedr, had the audacity to go to Mecca, where he sought to incite the Quraish to revenge by his sarcastic poems. Like most Arabs, Mohammed was especially sensitive to poetical satire. He did not easily forget vilifications of this sort. Among the comparatively few people who became the victims of his vengeance when he conquered his native city was a man who had composed contemptuous songs about him, and had them sung by two women in the wine-shops. The singers also were condemned to death, and one of them was actually executed. The same fate befell a professional singer of funeral dirges, who in addition to exercising her customary profession had dared to sing derogatory songs about Mohammed which others had taught her. For some reason she had been set free when she had fallen into the hands of the Prophet on a previous occasion. But on being convicted of persisting in her impudent course she had to pay the death-penalty. We should not forget that in Arabia at that time political satirical poetry was an especially deadly weapon. For a man like Mohammed, whose success depended to a large extent upon the esteem which he could win, a malicious satirical composition could be more dangerous than a lost battle. Even before this Ka'b had apparently made himself noticeable among those Jews who derided and heaped ridicule upon the revelation of the Prophet. After Ka'b returned to Medina in the spring of the year 3, Mohammed one day asked: 'Who will deliver me from Ka'b?' Mohammed Ibn Maslama and four other men volunteered. Mohammed gave them permission 'to say what they wished about him,' that is, to speak ill of him in order to coax the Jews into a trap; and he himself accompanied the murderers on the way to Ka'b's house.

Under the pretence that they were dissatisfied with Mohammed's rule, and contemplated a rebellion, Mohammed Ibn Maslama and his companions coaxed Ka'b out of his house, murdered him, and cast his bloody head at Mohammed's feet with the loud cry: 'Allah is great!' and the Prophet heartily agreed. Another Jew was disposed of in a similar manner. This Jew was a close friend of the elder brother of the murderer. For this reason the brother condemned the murder, accused the perpetrator of ingratitude, and said: 'Much of the fat on your body comes from the gifts of the Jews.' But the murderer answered: 'Verily, if the man who commanded me to kill that Jew should command me to kill you I would do so.' Then the brother replied: 'A religion which can drive men so far is an extraordinary religion,' and he was converted on the same day.[1] We see that Mohammed must have had an absolutely unique ability of winning people for his purposes, and of compelling them to regard other people and circumstances from his standpoint. What Allah's Apostle desires is just and good, even though it be fratricide.

In Mecca Mohammed's victory had provoked intense bitterness. A whole month passed before laments were sung for the dead, or offers made to redeem the prisoners. The motive was to deny Mohammed's triumph as long as possible. Abu Sufian swore that he would not anoint his head until he had obtained revenge. A little over a year passed, however, before the Quraish were ready to begin serious action against the enemy. In the month of Shawwal, in the year 3, a well-mounted and well-equipped army of 3,000 men, of whom 700 dressed in armour, departed from Mecca. A host of women followed the army in the belief that they would serve to spur on the fighting spirit of the warriors and remind them of those who fell at Bedr. Before the armies met the women marched before the army of the Meccans, singing to the accompaniment of tambourines, withdrawing later behind the

[1] Wakidi, p. 98.

host. Behind the lines they stopped those who were fleeing and urged them to return to the battle.

On this occasion also Mohammed exhibited noteworthy military talent. At first he thought it best to defend himself in the city, but the most warlike elements in his army, especially the young soldiers 'who swung their swords and raved like male camels,' convinced him that the enemy might construe this as cowardice. In military affairs Mohammed's authority was not always able to assert itself. Thus he was compelled to give in to them and leave the city. He then took up an advantageous position on the slopes of Uhud, three-fourths of a mile to the north of Medina. Here again he adhered strictly to the close battle formation. He arranged his men so that no shoulder should protrude from the ranks. He stationed the archers behind the army, and gave orders that under no conditions were they to move from their posts, but that they were to protect the battle formation against the flank attack of the hostile cavalry.

At first Mohammed was successful. The Quraish began to flee, and Abu Sufian himself was in danger of his life. Some of the believers moved forward to plunder the camp of the enemy. When they saw this the archers could no longer remain quiet, but rushed forward to share in the plunder. Khalid Ibn Al-Walid, who later became the famous general of the Islamic wars of conquest, used this opportunity to attack the Moslems in the rear. Suddenly the tables were turned. The believers began to flee in all directions. Mohammed tried in vain to stop them. He himself began to fight, and killed one of the enemy with his own hand. He was injured by a stone which knocked out a tooth, and smashed several of the rings of his coat-of-mail into his cheek. Then the Devil shouted that Mohammed had fallen, which increased the confusion in the Moslem ranks. Surrounded by his most loyal men, Mohammed slowly withdrew into the deep ravine which divides the black basalt mass of Mount Uhud. Abu Sufian shouted several scornful remarks into the ravine to the Moslems, and Umar answered with equal vigour. Then the Quraish began to withdraw without making a real attempt to exploit their victory. It seems remarkable that it did not occur to them to attack the city itself. This proves that the conflict was still directed against Mohammed, and not Medina, where a considerable proportion of the population, and especially the Jews, was still openly hostile or cool toward the new prophet. Before the army departed the battlefield was searched and the dead were robbed and mutilated. The women raved like furies. Hind, the wife of Sufian, went ahead and cut off the noses and ears of the dead. Among the dead was the heroic Hamza, the uncle of the Prophet, who had killed Hind's father at Bedr. His murderer left the liver of the dead man for Hind, who bit into it and spat the pieces out around her. She wore the severed nose and ears of Hamza as an ornament. When the believers finally recovered Hamza's mutilated corpse the Prophet declared that his name was recorded in Paradise as 'the lion of Allah and His Apostle.'

Owing to the lack of aggressiveness and the folly of the enemy, Mohammed and his followers were not only able to return to the city in good order, but on the following day, although tired and weakened by his wounds, he could even undertake a semblance of pursuit of the enemy, in order to obliterate the bad impression which the defeat had made upon his opponents and rivals in Medina. However, the battle of Uhud was of no decisive importance for Mohammed's position. For a time his prestige seemed to be waning. The 'hypocrites'—as Mohammed called the people of Medina who remained indifferent to his prophetic claims—openly expressed their malicious joy, and the Jews insisted that Mohammed was only striving for political power, for it was an unheard-of thing for a prophet to be injured in battle in this fashion. The Bedouin in Bir Ma'una even dared to massacre forty Koran reciters whom Mohammed had sent to them as missionaries. But the Prophet's endurance, and the loyalty of his followers, gradually turned the tide again in his favour. The tradition records many touching examples of the heroism and sacrificial spirit of Mohammed's early companions. This proves that the success of Islam—although it has been said, and with some justification, that his triumph was essentially conditioned by the love of adventure and desire for plunder of the Bedouin—was also partly due to the fact that he had really been able to make effective genuinely profound ideals and moral powers.

The continued strife with the Jews provided the faithful with a convenient opportunity for replenishing their fortune. Barely one year after the battle of Uhud, Mohammed disposed of the second Jewish tribe, Banu Nadir. After the Jews had been besieged for a while they were permitted to withdraw unmolested. They departed to the accompaniment of drums and the music of strings. Their wives were decked in festive costumes, and they dazzled the warriors of the Prophet by their beauty and elegance. A people that could not be crushed! The tribe of Banu Nadir migrated to Khaibar, fifteen miles north of Medina, and the plantations which they had possessed in Medina were divided among the emigrants.

In the following year, the fifth after the Hegira, an event occurred in the private life of the Prophet which, perhaps more than anything else, has provoked the unfavourable judgment of Mohammed's personality which prevails to this day in the West. The story is as follows: Mohammed had an adopted son, Zaid Ibn Haritha, an Arabian slave who had been presented to Khadijah by a relative shortly after their wedding. Mohammed formed a friendship with the slave, got possession of him as a present from his wife, and then set him free. He married him to Umm Aiman, a slave who was almost the only possession which he had received from his mother. At this time Umm Aiman must have been considerably over forty years old, and Mohammed was apparently grateful to Zaid for wanting to make her happy. He is said to have promised him Paradise because he married her. Zaid was one of the first to embrace Islam, in fact the third after Khadijah and Ali. He had stood loyally by his foster-father, was highly respected by him, and had been in command in a number of military raids. Of course, he had also a younger wife. She was Zainab bint Jahsh, a cousin of the Prophet. She is supposed—but apparently this judgment applies to her later years—to have been deeply pious. In order to remain standing in prayer as long as possible she is said to have hung a rope in the mosque as a support. She was handy, cured hides, made shoes, and gave the income from her work to the poor.[1] Above all she was beautiful, and apparently rather proud and ambitious.

One day the Prophet came to Zaid's house as was his frequent custom.[2] Zaid was not at home, but Zainab met him at the door, clad in the light garment which the Arab women used to wear in the house. Mohammed was overcome with amazement at her beauty, and he said, half-audibly, as he drew back courteously: 'Praised be Allah who changeth the hearts of men!' But Zainab had heard his words, and she repeated them to Zaid. The possibility of being elevated to the position of the wife of the Prophet certainly appealed to her proud nature. Her husband was hardly attractive, at least externally. He was small, black-skinned and flat-nosed. We can imagine that Zainab told poor Zaid so often about the impression which she had made upon the Prophet that he, as the tradition has it, finally felt repulsed by her. So he went to Mohammed and volunteered to divorce Zainab, so that the Prophet might marry her. Owing to his fear of public opinion Mohammed did not wish to accept this offer. For Zaid was his adopted son, although, only six years younger than Mohammed, and the Arabs regarded an adopted son as in every respect equal to a natural son, and thus a marriage between a foster-father and the divorced wife would be looked upon as incest. Finally a revelation was received which removed the Prophet's doubts. One day when he was with 'Ayesha the inspiration came upon him, and on awakening he said: 'Who will go to Zainab and congratulate her because Allah has given her to me in marriage?' The revelation in question is found in Sura 33, 37. There it reads: 'And remember the time when thou saidst to him unto whom

[1] Ibn Sa'd, viii, p. 9.

[2] Tabari, i, pp. 1460 ff.

God had shown favour, and to whom thou also hadst shown favour,"Keep thy wife to thyself, and fear God"; and thou didst hide in thy mind what God would bring to light, and thou didst fear man; but more right had it been to fear God. And when Zaid had settled concerning her to divorce her, we married her to thee, that it might not be a crime in the faithful to marry the wives of their adopted sons, when they have settled the affair concerning them. And the behest of God is to be performed.' When this Koran verse was revealed, 'Ayesha, with her ready wit, is supposed to have said: 'Truly thy Lord makes haste to do thy pleasure.' Another time she said pointedly that this verse proves that Mohammed never suppressed the revelations which he received, for if he had been compelled to suppress one it would have been this one.[1] A tradition which does not censor such statements must apparently possess a high degree of historical trustworthiness. The fact that they were preserved proves also that Mohammed's conduct in this affair was not regarded as a serious error.

So Mohammed married Zainab, and she was very proud that she had reached the goal of her desires. She used to boast that Allah Himself was her *wali* (matchmaker), saying: The other wives of the Prophet were given to him in marriage by their families, but Allah Himself gave me to him in the highest heaven.[2] This affair with Zainab did not in the least disturb the good relationship between Mohammed and Zaid. The latter still enjoyed the full confidence of the Prophet, and seems to have merited it in every respect. Like other adherents of the Prophet he married several times, and had himself divorced, apparently regarding his divorce more in the light of a business transaction than as a love tragedy.

That same year the Quraish finally realized the necessity of trying, with all their strength, to crush Mohammed's growing power. This time they came with an army that is supposed to have comprised no less than ten thousand

[1] Ahmed ibn Hanbal, *Musnad*, i, p. 63.
[2] Zad al-ma'ad, i, p. 27.

men, intending to attack the enemy in the city itself. But Mohammed quickly put Medina in a state of readiness for defence. Here his superior gifts and his ready grasp of the situation again came to his aid. Upon the advice of a Persian he had the unprotected parts of the city surrounded by a moat and a wall. In spite of its crude nature this means of defence, comparatively unfamiliar to the Arabs, seems to have fulfilled its purpose. The Meccans did not attempt an attack. Finally they grew tired of the siege, and departed without having accomplished anything by their magnificently planned campaign.

In the course of the siege Mohammed became aware of the danger which he would incur if he were to have a dangerous enemy within the confines of his own city in a time of crisis. So, as an example, he decided to punish the last of the Jewish tribes, Banu Karaiza, for the lack of dependability which it had shown during the siege. On this occasion he again revealed that lack of honesty and moral courage which was an unattractive trait in his character. The Banu Karaiza had formerly been allied with one of the Arabic tribes in Medina, the Aus, and a consideration for the feeling of obligation which the Aus still had toward their old allies forced the Prophet to proceed with caution. So he asked them if they would agree if he were to appoint a man of their own tribe to decide the fate of the Jews, and they naturally accepted joyfully. Then Mohammed delegated the decision to Sa‘d Ibn Mu‘adh, one of his most fanatical followers, who had been wounded during the siege, and now lay dying. The Prophet knew what he was doing. Sa‘d's verdict was that all the men of the tribe should be put to the sword, and all the women and children should be sold in slavery. And this inhuman verdict was executed without mercy. One must see Mohammed's cruelty toward the Jews against the background of the fact that their scorn and rejection was the greatest disappointment of his life, and for a time they threatened completely to destroy his prophetic authority. For him, therefore, it was a fixed axiom that the

Jews were the sworn enemies of Allah and His revelation. Any mercy toward them was out of the question.

In the following years Mohammed's power increased slowly but surely. More and more the calculating Bedouin, to whom his religious views had seemed rather strange, began to cast their eyes upon the ruler of Medina and to seek his friendship. In one of the sacred months of the year 6 (March, A.D. 628) Mohammed decided to make the pilgrimage to Mecca. Perhaps he reasoned that in view of his growing power among the Arabian tribes the Quraish would not venture to deny him access to the Ka'ba, or that they would not dare to violate the peace of the sacred months as he himself had done. At any rate, he wanted to give the Arabs who had come together for the pilgrimage an imposing demonstration of his power, and of the influence which he had already attained. In order to compel respect he sent a challenge to those Bedouin tribes with whom he was on good terms to accompany him on the pilgrimage. However, the Bedouin regarded the plan as too daring, and refused to join him.

Nevertheless, Mohammed made the journey with a thousand followers. Armed only with swords, they were in a state of *ihram*. Consequently they were subjected to the restrictions of freedom of action which this holy state imposed upon them. Therefore it is hardly believable that Mohammed at first thought of attacking Mecca. However, the Quraish had ascertained that Mohammed was approaching, and 'they made a compact with Allah' that they would under no circumstances allow him to enter the city. They sent Khalid Ibn Al-Walid ahead with two hundred riders to ascertain what he intended to do. The remainder of the men also went out, and women and children followed the army. Mohammed now exhibited something of that recklessness which he could display when he was in deadly earnest. He suggested to his confidants that they should attack the city. But Abu Bekr was of the opinion that they ought to go right ahead and think only of the pilgrimage, as had been previously decided, and to resort to their weapons only in case the

Quraish definitely tried to prevent them. For, from the Arabic point of view Mohammed's suggestion implied a very serious infraction of the law. It involved not only the violation of the sanctity of the pilgrimage months, but also an offence against the sacred and protected territory of Mecca. However, the Prophet replied that Khalid had already advanced against the believers with his riders, and that therefore the conflict had actually already begun.[1] Here the narrator inserts the remark that Mohammed always asked for the opinion of others when he was on campaign, a thing which he did not do otherwise. On this occasion he had to give in to Abu Bekr's opinion.

When Khalid, with his riders in battle order, came to a halt directly in front of the believers, the hour of prayer had just arrived. Then Mohammed introduced the special prayer which was later sanctioned by the revelation under the name of 'the prayer during fear.' Usually the army was in the habit of praying together as a unit, but now it was divided into sections, one of which faced toward the enemy while the other prayed. Even those who prayed did not lay their weapons aside. The following night Mohammed, with the help of a guide, caused the army to travel through almost inaccessible mountain passes to Hudaibiyya, three miles north of Mecca, where he pitched camp. On the way it happened that Mohammed's camel fell on its knees and lay down. His companions thought that the animal was fatigued, and was unable to proceed, but the Prophet said: 'No, there is something which prevents it. It is the same thing which prevented the elephants from reaching Mecca.' It seems thus that Mohammed had already thought of retreat, and was trying to explain the failure to himself and to others, on the grounds that Allah Himself did not wish to have him come to His sanctuary at this time.

The Quraish now sent various messengers to Mohammed, to discover what he had in mind. One of them, a Quraishite named 'Urwa, returned very greatly impressed by the rever-

[1] Wakidi, p. 244.

ence, not to speak of worship, which the believers paid to their Prophet. As he declared, they did not dare to speak loudly in his presence. He only needed to move a hand, and everything that he desired was carried out. They smeared their bodies with his spittle and fought one another to obtain the water with which he had washed. They valued their life as of no account when it was a matter of protecting him, and even their women would in no way betray him.

Nevertheless, the Quraish hardly seemed to make any attempt to carry on actual negotiations with Mohammed. Their messengers seemed to be more in the nature of spies. Mohammed's behaviour toward one of them is of some interest for the evaluation of his character. He was a Bedouin chief, Hulais Ibn Alkama, whom the Meccans had sent to Hudaibiyya. When Mohammed saw him coming he said: 'He is one of those who set great value upon being pious.' So he had the sacrificial camels driven out of the side valley where they had been tied. They came, decked in their neckbands, which showed that they were designated for sacrifice, and they had chewed off their own wool because they had been tied up so long. When Hulais saw this he did not come near to Mohammed, but turned back in reverence because of what he had seen, and told the Quraish of Mohammed's pious intentions. They taunted him and told him that he was a Bedouin devoid of sense, but Hulais insisted that his compact with the Quraish did not involve the exclusion from Allah's house of one who had come pay Him reverence.[1] Thus we see that Mohammed, who was ready to attack the city, which was situated in Allah's protected territory, could now exploit the simple-hearted Bedouin's pious reverence for the sacred area.

In the meantime Mohammed sent his own son-in-law, Uthman Ibn 'Affan, to Mecca in order to come to an agreement. When after three days he did not return the worst was feared. Then Mohammed gathered his followers about

[1] Wakidi, p. 252.

him, and had them take a solemn oath not to flee, and, if necessary, to die for the Prophet. This oath of allegiance, as the tradition terms it, was received by Mohammed as he sat under a green tree. He must have understood how to make this ceremony genuinely impressive and to exploit to the full the reverence and devotion which he had awakened in his followers. The oath was confirmed by a hand-clasp. The first man who came forward was a man named Sinan. He said, as he gripped the hand of the Prophet: 'I swear to stand by you in all that you may wish to undertake.' Right or wrong, my Prophet!—an eloquent testimony to the power which religious leaders are able to win over their adherents.

This oath of allegiance kindled a glowing enthusiasm among the Moslems. They were firmly resolved to attack the Meccan forces should they really attempt to exclude the believers from the sanctuary. Finally, as a reply to Uthman's embassy, three negotiators arrived, among them Suhail, one of the chief enemies of Mohammed. They had received instructions to try to reach a peaceful agreement with Mohammed, to the effect that he should not visit the temple that year but should receive, in return, permission to come again the next year, and perform the ceremonies of the pilgrimage. They did not wish to have it said in Arabia that Mohammed had gained entrance to the temple by force. Thus, if in Mecca the situation was felt to be rather serious, at all events everything had been done to preserve appearances. However, the advent of the negotiators did not signify that the Quraish regarded themselves as the weaker party. Suhail had a long conference with Mohammed, with the result that subject to certain conditions a ten years' armistice was agreed upon. The idea of a truce seemed to come from the Prophet himself. In the agreement it was stipulated that Mohammed should not enter Mecca that year. In the following year the Meccans were to evacuate their city for three days, in order to permit Mohammed and his followers to carry out the pilgrimage. During the period of the ten years' armistice both parties were free to make whatever alliances they desired. Mohammed agreed to return any members of the Quraish under age who might flee to him after the termination of the armistice. There was no corresponding obligation for the Quraish. At the final formulation and signing of the pact Mohammed yielded to an act of disrespect on the part of Suhail, which can only be explained by assuming that it was Mohammed who really initiated the armistice rather than the Quraish. Ali was supposed to write the agreement. Mohammed dictated it according to the customary Islamic formula: 'In the name of Allah, the Compassionate, the Merciful.' Suhail claimed that the Compassionate was a God whom he did not know, and that the formula should read, as was customary in Mecca: 'In Thy name, O Thou, our God.' Mohammed acquiesced, although the Moslems murmured audibly. He continued with his dictation: 'A peace pact between Mohammed, the Apostle of Allah, and Suhail.' Suhail interrupted him and reminded him that he did not acknowledge Mohammed as the Apostle of Allah. Mohammed yielded at once, and dictated: 'Mohammed Ibn Abdallah.'

The Prophet's action was a terrible disappointment to his followers, who had just vowed, with glowing enthusiasm, to die for him and his cause. Such a disgraceful agreement seemed almost like submission. The brave and honest Umar was raving. He rushed up to the Prophet and shouted: 'Are we not Moslems? Then why do we yield in a matter pertaining to our faith?' Mohammed tried in vain to subdue him with an authoritative command that he was Allah's Apostle, and that he did nothing unless Allah revealed it. Umar turned excitedly to Abu Bekr and other leaders who were near the Prophet, to ascertain whether they really intended to submit to this humiliation. He declared later that never before had he had such doubts concerning Mohammed's truthfulness, and if he had found merely a hundred like-minded men, he would have resigned from the *umma* of Islam.[1]

Events proved, however, that the Prophet had acted wisely.

[1] Wakidi, p. 255.

To what extent he himself foresaw and aimed at the consequences of this agreement is not absolutely clear. But it is probable that Mohammed himself, who apparently felt the strong and mysterious attraction which the rites of Mecca's national sanctuary had for the Arabs, realized that a state of warfare with the Quraish would to a certain extent bar him from the fellowship which, no matter how weak and indefinite, was nevertheless symbolized by the observance of the sacred months, the pilgrimage, and the markets around Mecca. It is certain that the Bedouin tribes would have definitely hesitated to enter into an open alliance with Mohammed as long as he was in conflict with the Quraish, and that this was not merely due to their fear of the military power of Mecca. Immediately after the acceptance of this armistice, the Khoza'a tribes along the coast, who were secretly already on his side, came forward and openly confessed themselves to be Mohammed's allies. And their example was soon followed by many other tribes, so that even Umar was compelled to admit that more people had embraced Islam as a result of the armistice than in the whole preceding period. Abu Bekr declared that no victory had brought so many adherents to Islam as the armistice of Hudaibiyya.

It is obvious that these conversions were not always due to purely religious reasons. Among those who came to Medina to embrace Islam were also married women, who, according to older Arabian views, were classed as minors, and thus were to be surrendered according to the agreement. In Sura 60, 10 Allah commands the Prophet to examine these new converts, and if it is established that they are really sincere in their faith, they are to be kept and not returned to the unbelievers. On the other hand, believers who had heathen wives were to send them back to their families. Presumably the tests of faith to which the new converts were subjected were not excessively strict, but that they were demanded at all shows that in many cases conversion notoriously occurred because of other than genuinely religious reasons. To those women of Mecca who lived in less fortunate family circumstances, or who had a pronounced liking for romantic adventures, an escape to Medina offered alluring prospects. But no doubt personal conviction was often involved. The Arabian women often showed that they did not weakly conform with the opinions of their husbands or relatives, but accepted Islam independently, and because of personal preferences. Abu Sufian's own daughter, Umm Habiba, was a true believer. She migrated to Abyssinia, where she became a widow, and later she married the Prophet himself. It is said that when her father came to Mecca as an envoy, and visited the house of his daughter, he started to sit upon a mat when Umm Habiba declared that no unclean idolater could sit upon a mat belonging to Allah's Apostle. On the other hand, even Umar still had two wives who were heathen, and he divorced them at this time.

In the following year (7) Mohammed instituted a campaign against the Jews in Khaibar, which again yielded rich booty. Among other things a camel's skin full of jewels and ornaments was taken, a treasure belonging to a family which used to loan it out as a wedding adornment over a large part of Arabia. Before the division of the plunder Mohammed gave a pearl necklace from this treasure to 'Ayesha. But the fact that he had thus taken more than his legitimate share caused him a sleepless night. The next day he wanted to have the necklace returned, but he discovered that 'Ayesha had already distributed the pearls among the poor[1] The frankness with which this error is acknowledged does credit both to Mohammed and to the Moslem tradition.

At Khaibar Mohammed increased his harem by another wife, the ninth. This was Safiya, a beautiful Jewess who belonged to one of the tribes driven from Medina, but who nevertheless, apparently, felt flattered to become the wife of the Prophet. Evidently the women of that day usually accepted with great complacency the fate which passed them on from one hand to another, as living and circulating trophies of the incessantly changing conflicts. Another Jewess whose

[1] Wakidi, p. 278.

father, uncle, and husband had been killed by the Moslems, proved more loyal to her people and her religion. She presented Mohammed with a roast lamb which she had poisoned. However, the Prophet discovered the plot in time, and good-naturedly pardoned the culprit.

The self-control which Mohammed revealed at Hudaibiyya, his ability to bear occasional humiliation in unimportant issues, in order to achieve an exalted goal, shows that he was a person of unique ability. A man of his mental superiority always keeps the reins in his hands, even when he is forced to yield for the moment. And the time soon came when he was able to reap the fruits of the wisdom which he displayed at Hudaibiyya. Two Bedouin tribes, one of which, the Khoza'a, was allied to Mohammed, and the other, Banu Bekr, to the Quraish, had come into mutual conflict. The Banu Bekr succeeded in obtaining a promise from several of the Quraish that they would supply them with weapons and cavalry for their struggle against Mohammed's allies. The promise is said to have been made without Abu Sufian's consent. But since Khalid Ibn Al-Walid and other prominent leaders had already gone over to Mohammed, and since there was a growing peace party in Mecca, which wanted to remain on good terms with the Prophet, Abu Sufian began to fear Mohammed's growing power, and he is supposed to have gone to Medina in the attempt to smooth matters out again. The stories of the role which Abu Sufian played in the last phase of Mohammed's conflict with his countrymen are partially contradictory, but it is certain that even before the fall of the city the leading men of Mecca had gone over to the side of the victor.

Mohammed now began to prepare for a gigantic expedition. He kept his plans absolutely secret. It is an indication of his authority over his followers that not even his most trusted companions knew anything about his intentions. Abu Bekr himself tried to question his daughter 'Ayesha, while she was busy preparing the Prophet's supplies for the journey, but he learned nothing. Finally Mohammed himself told his friend that he intended to fight the Quraish because they had broken the truce by attacking one of his allies. But Abu Bekr was pledged to absolute silence. In order to divert attention from his real purpose Mohammed sent out a little reconnoitring patrol against an opposing Bedouin tribe.

On Wednesday the 10th of Ramadan in the year 8 (January, A.D. 630) Mohammed departed from Medina with an army of ten thousand men.[1] He stated that those who wished might break the fast, but that those who did not wish to do so might keep it. It was not until they were under way that it became evident that the expedition was aimed at Mecca. In the native city of the Prophet the rumour of his departure from Medina apparently caused intense restlessness. Abu Sufian now went out to meet Mohammed in the hope of beginning negotiations. According to one account Mohammed repeatedly rejected his former enemy in proud silence, until finally Abu Sufian took his son by the hand, and declared that if Mohammed remained adamant he would take his son and wander about in the desert until they had both perished of hunger and thirst. Not until then did Mohammed accept the confession of faith which Abu Sufian wanted to make. In this naïve fashion the later legend satisfies its desire for revenge against the man who had offered such persistent opposition to the Prophet. But such conduct is absolutely alien to Mohammed's character. He always made a special effort, by means of magnanimity and conciliation, to win over precisely the most able and important of his enemies. Moreover, a man of such nobility as Abu Sufian would never have submitted to such humiliation. Another tradition, which states that Abu Sufian and two other men had been sent out by their countrymen as investigators and negotiators, is no doubt nearer to the truth. When he saw Mohammed's growing power he seemed to have realized the folly of continued resistance, and decided to change his alliance. Presumably this did not happen without friendly persuasion on Mohammed's part. It is said that when he

[1] For the following compare Wakidi, pp. 325-354.

was supposed to confess the statement of belief he frankly stated that the first part, 'there is no God but Allah,' presented no difficulties for him, but that he still doubted the second part, 'Mohammed is Allah's Prophet.' He succeeded, however, in conquering his doubts, and on returning to his countrymen he advised them to remain in their houses and not to attempt resistance.

So Mohammed entered Mecca with practically no opposition. Only Suhail and 'Ikrima, Abu Jahl's son, attempted to resist him with a handful of followers. Khalid and his riders scattered them and chased them high up into the mountains. Thus Mohammed conquered the very city which he had deserted as a refugee eight years before. After he had rested for a while and had performed his ablutions, he went to the Ka'ba fully armed with Abu Bekr at his side. When he arrived at the sanctuary he touched the black stone with his staff and broke forth into an *Allahu-akbar*, 'God is great,' which spread like a mighty chorus throughout the whole army of the Moslems. Then he rode once around the Ka'ba, descended from his camel, and asked for the key to the sanctuary. He destroyed the idols inside and outside the building, especially Hubal's image, which stood directly facing the entrance. Then the Prophet, leaning against the doorpost of the Ka'ba with the key in his hands, spoke to the assembled Moslems. He said that the day of paganism was past, and that all blood-guilt, debts, and other obligations of a pagan period were now obsolete. Likewise all privileges were now cancelled. 'Now Allah is finished with pride of position. You are all descended from Adam, and the best man among you is the most pious.' He emphasized the sanctity of Mecca's sanctuary: 'No man before me was permitted to injure this sacred place, and no man after me shall do it. I myself have only been permitted to do it during a part of one day.' In this respect the followers of the Prophet have been more obedient to his example than to his word, and more than once Mecca became the scene of bloody warfare. In the rebellion against Yazid in the year 64 (A.D. 683) things went so far that the Ka'ba was set on fire. On the other hand, those followers of the Prophet who were zealously obedient to the law became all the more strict. Some maintained that not even the vegetables that had been grown in a garden in Mecca might be consumed, and that it was unlawful to allow horses or camels to graze within the area of the city. Others ruled that no rent could be charged for the houses in Mecca, and that the rooms that were available must be offered gratis to the pilgrims. The Caliph Umar is said to have decreed that the inhabitants of the city were forbidden to lock their doors, for the pilgrims should be able to stay wherever they please. These were, of course, pious wishes which were never realized.

It is rarely that a victor has exploited his victory with greater self-restraint and forbearance than did Mohammed. Only ten persons were placed upon the list of the proscribed. I have already mentioned the three singers. Some of the remainder, who had committed murder and had escaped punishment by flight, were now executed without further ceremony. Another man, who barely escaped death by a hair's breadth, was Abdallah Ibn Sa'd. He had indulged in a jest with reference to Mohammed's revelations which might have become very disastrous to the Prophet. In writing down the revelations according to Mohammed's dictation, he had inserted slight changes to see whether this would be noticed. When the Prophet dictated 'Allah is knowing and hearing' (*'alimun sami'un*), Abdallah substituted the words: 'Knowing and wise' (*'alimun hakīmun*). When Mohammed failed to notice this he began to doubt whether the Prophet could ever distinguish the revelations from his own notions. He therefore deserted Islam and returned to Mecca. At the request of Uthman, Abdallah Ibn Sa'd was pardoned.[1] Another man had cruelly mistreated Mohammed's daughter Zainab, when she fled to Medina after the battle of Bedr. Because he repented he was pardoned. Hind also was condemned to death for mutilating the corpse of Hamza, but she was pardoned

[1] Wakidi, p. 345; Ibn Hisham, ii, p. 239.

because she embraced Islam. Mohammed's treatment of those enemies who had been the moving spirits of Mecca's long conflict with him is very noteworthy. Only one of them, namely 'Iqrima, was on the black list. He saved himself by flight, but when later he returned repentant Mohammed received him with friendliness, and forbade his men to defame 'Iqrima's father, Mohammed's deadly foe Abu Jahl, since the defaming of the dead is an unnecessary slandering of their descendants. By special amiability Mohammed sought to win over the remainder of those who had opposed him. Suhail, who had vilified him so unmercifully at Hudaibiyya, locked himself up in his house, full of dark forebodings, and sent his son Abdallah to the conqueror to sue for mercy. Mohammed forgave Suhail and decreed: 'None of you are permitted to show an evil countenance to Suhail, for a man of such noble birth and good sense cannot long remain hostile to Islam.' Another of his opponents, Safwan, received a safe conduct for four months, since he was not willing to accept Islam immediately. During this time he accompanied the Prophet upon his expedition against the Hawazin tribes, and once he noticed among the captured booty a splendid herd of sheep and camels, which had been driven into a ravine. Mohammed saw his glances, and asked him whether the herd pleased him. When he answered in the affirmative, Mohammed presented all the animals to him. Impressed by such generosity, Safwan accepted Islam. On the whole, this caused much murmuring among the oldest and most loyal of Mohammed's followers, for in the last and very profitable expedition practically all the booty had been reserved for the recent converts, who were still, in the eyes of the veterans, only semi-pagans. Mohammed declared this to be necessary in order 'to arouse confidence in their hearts.' The gain to his religion acquired in this fashion was more than doubtful. But his position as a ruler was strengthened by his generosity, and his ability to set personal opinions and feelings aside in order to reach larger goals. Especially when important personalities were involved, who could be of service to his cause, Mohammed showed an astonishing power of freeing himself from all resentment, and evaluating people exclusively from the standpoint of their actual worth. In spite of all his winsome amiability, this element of objectivity often lends to his personality a certain quality of cold calculation.

In the month of Rabi'al-awwal in the year 9, Mohammed undertook an expedition to Tabuq in North-west Arabia. According to Wakidi, this move was called forth by the rumour that the Emperor Heraclius was gathering a tremendous army in Syria with a view to attacking the new ruler of Hejaz. Mohammed regarded the danger to be so serious that this time, in opposition to his usual custom, he informed his men concerning the object of the mobilization, and appealed to the believers to make contributions toward the equipment of the army. That he attached great importance to the coming conflict is shown also by the fact that the campaign was undertaken at a time when it was not customary to indulge in short raids. The first harvest was approaching, and the terrific heat excluded the possibility of long marches. Nevertheless, the real purpose of the expedition is not quite clear. It may be left open to doubt whether Mohammed sought only to liberate and convert the troops of the Emperor by a victory over the Arabian tribe who were under the domination of Byzantium,[1] or whether the definite idea had already occurred to him that Islam, as a religion, and thus he himself, was destined to expand his rule beyond the boundaries of the Arabian peninsula. The latter possibility should not be disregarded. It is a striking fact that the Prophet who in Mecca often declared that it was his task to give his people an Arabian Koran, a revelation specifically intended for the Arabic nation, did not revert to this idea in Medina. Abraham's religion, which Mohammed, after his conflict with the Jews, interpreted as the specifically pure and original revelation, in opposition to the falsified scriptural religions, contained within itself

[1] But compare also Buhl, *Das Leben Muhammeds*, Leipzig, 1930, p. 323.

a universal purpose, and if for the time being it tolerated the simultaneous existence of Judaism and Christianity, this was only a *modus vivendi,* an admission of the relative precedence which these religions enjoyed in relation to Arabian paganism. A proud belief in the future of his religion dominates the soul of the Prophet: 'He it is who hath sent His Apostle with guidance and a religion of the truth, that He may make it victorious over every other religion, albeit they who assign partners to God be averse from it' (9, 33). For the time being his struggle was with the People of the Book 'who forbid not that which God and His Apostle have forbidden, and who profess not the profession of the truth,' only in order to force them to submit and pay taxes (9, 29). Thus they are permitted to retain their religion. This was the policy which Islam was to adopt in the future with regard to the Biblical religions.

However, on account of the heat, in which only night marches were possible, the expedition to Syria, undertaken with an army of thirty thousand men, was an ill-considered venture. Mohammed was forced to turn back at Tabuq, forty miles north of Medina. Nevertheless, the expedition was not entirely fruitless, since a number of petty Christian princes, among others John of 'Aila, surrendered and paid tribute to the Prophet.

During his last years in Medina Mohammed's sovereignty embraced practically the whole of Arabia. A large number of tribes sent emissaries to him, and voluntarily accepted Islam, while others submitted only after military pressure. As a rule Mohammed seems to have made formal treaties with every single tribe. Arabian historians record a number of the texts of such treaties. As an example we may cite the agreement with Banu Harith Ibn Ka'b, a tribe of Southern Arabia.[1] Mohammed ordered that the new converts should be instructed in the Koran by a specially delegated missionary; they were to be taught the truth about Paradise and Hell, and how to offer prayer in the proper manner. Among pagan

[1] Ibn Sa'd, i, 2, p. 102.

customs the Prophet especially prohibited the wearing of garments which were too light, and the custom of calling upon 'the tribes and families' in battle, i.e. ancestor worship. Legal alms constituted one-tenth of all naturally irrigated acreage, one-twentieth of all artificially irrigated acreage, and a payment of live-stock consisting of two sheep for every ten camels owned.

The South Arabian Christians in Nejran also sent an emissary to the Prophet and submitted to his rule.[1] The Nejranites were compelled to pay a rather high tribute: two thousand garments worth each an ounce of silver. In return their life, possessions, and religion were to enjoy the Prophet's protection. No bishop was to be driven from his see nor any monk from his cell. In addition the Nejranites must pledge themselves not to practise usury, which meant in this case they were forbidden to take interest upon loans. The commandment which Mohammed here applied to the Christians had already been accepted as a recognized moral obligation in the Nestorian Church, unconditionally enforced upon the priests and clerics, and which the synodical statutes, as far as possible, sought to recommend to the laity as an admonition of the Gospel, without making it an absolute law.

In the following year Mohammed made the sacred pilgrimage to Mecca, fulfilling for the first and only time the ritual which he himself had prescribed. Seated upon the back of his camel he again addressed his followers. He reminded them of the new regulations which he had given concerning the reckoning of time. He declared that a cycle was now completed, and that they had again arrived at the point corresponding to Allah's creation of heaven and earth. Whether these words were really spoken by the Prophet, or whether they reflect the ideas of the early congregation concerning their Prophet, they do reproduce very ancient conceptions of a new era, a new age which begins with good fortune and happiness for humanity because a new ruler has come to power. In addition Mohammed insisted that

[1] *Ibid.*, p. 84.

usury and blood-vengeance must be abolished. The Prophet also spoke of the position of women. As compared with men they are like prisoners of war and have no jurisdiction over themselves, nor have they any right to follow their own preferences in the matter of receiving visitors in their homes. When they rebel their husbands have a right to punish them with moderation, but they must be treated with kindness and justice under the fear of Allah. The Prophet commanded them to treat all Moslems as brothers. No believer must injure the life or property of his brother. His followers should fight all others until they confessed: 'There is no God but Allah.'

Several months after his return from the 'farewell pilgrimage,' as it was called, the Prophet contracted a dangerous fever. One night he awakened his liberated slave, Abu Muwaihaba, and told him that he had received the command to go to one of the cemeteries of Medina to pray for the departed. So they went to the cemetery, where Mohammed prayed: 'Peace be with you, people of the graves! You are surely happier than the living. For temptations shall come upon men like thieves in a dark night, the last more evil than the first.' Then, according to pious tradition, he is supposed to have said: 'O Abu Muwaihaba! Allah offered me the key of the world and prophesied long life and Paradise thereafter, and allowed me to choose whether I desired this or to meet my Lord at once. I have chosen the latter.'[1]

In Mohammed's case the premonition of death, which so frequently precedes a serious illness, and is perhaps caused by a vague physical sense of the hidden workings of destructive powers, found expression on the occasion of his nocturnal visit to the cemetery. Immediately after his return the Prophet's illness began. He found 'Ayesha suffering with a headache. When she complained, 'My head, my head!' Mohammed replied, 'I would have more reason to say my head, my head! Besides, if you were to die before me, what would it matter to you? I would wrap you in a shroud,

[1] Ibn Hisham, ii, p. 422.

pray over you, and bury you!' 'Ayesha attempted to assume the jesting tone which she so often employed in the presence of her exalted husband, and said: 'I think I can imagine how you would come home after such a performance, and immediately celebrate a wedding with a new wife.' The Prophet smiled at her jest.

When Mohammed's condition became worse he asked his other wives for permission to remain in 'Ayesha's house. When his pain became intense he was given a drug which was considered especially efficacious in cases of inflammation of the lungs. Mohammed awoke and asked bitterly who had given him the drug, and gave orders that as a punishment for their deed all his wives were to take the same dose. It seems that the sickness was slightly relieved, so that the Prophet was able again to appear in the mosque, where, according to his decree, Abu Bekr led the prayers. But the hopes of his recovery proved deceptive. The fever returned with renewed force. On the 13th of the month Rabi'al-awwal (June 8, 632), with his head resting in 'Ayesha's lap, he breathed his last. 'No, the friend, the highest in Paradise'[1]—were the last words heard from his lips.

[1] Buhl, 354, note 95.

CHAPTER VII

Mohammed's Personality

DANTE consigns Mohammed, with his body split from the head down to the waist, to the twenty-eighth sphere of the Inferno, and shows him tearing apart his severed breast with his own hands, because he is the chief among the damned souls who have brought schism into religion. Mohammed's crime was the espousing of a false religion. To the medieval mind his claim to deliver a Divine revelation which was to supersede Christianity could only be regarded as an impious fraud. Even to-day Mohammed is primarily 'the false Prophet' in the eyes of a more naïve Christian polemic.

The concepts of the period of Enlightenment permitted a more just estimate of Mohammed's personality. In their naïve fashion the thinkers of this period often evaluated the outstanding wisdom and virtue of ancient lawgivers and founders of religions, and stressed the reasonableness of alien faiths, praising them at the expense of Christianity. They extended to Islam this benevolent evaluation of the non-Christian religions. Sale, who in 1734 published a translation of the Koran which for long remained the standard version, compared Mohammed with Numa and Theseus. A few years previously De Boulainvilliers had written a *Life of Mohammed* with the avowed purpose of demonstrating the superiority of Islam to Christianity. He portrayed Mohammed as a wise and enlightened lawgiver, who sought to establish a reasonable religion in place of the dubious dogmas of Judaism and Christianity. The same attitude is expressed in Savary's translation of the Koran, which was published in 1752. He regards Mohammed as one of those unusual personalities occasionally appearing in history, who remake their environment and enlist men in their triumphant train. Savary thinks that anyone studying Mohammed's career must marvel at the achievements of which human genius is capable when circumstances are favourable. Although born as an idolater, Mohammed rose to the worship of one God. In the course of his travels he observed how the divided Christians poured condemnation upon one another, and how the Jews, 'the scum of the nations,' obstinately clung to their laws. In contrast with this Mohammed sought to establish a new universal religion, by setting up a simple dogma which contained only what the reason must accept, namely, belief in one God who rewards virtue and punishes transgressors. But in order to move men to accept this doctrine, Savary thinks, he had to claim Divine authority. So he demanded that he should be accepted as the Apostle of Allah, this being a pious fraud dictated by rational necessity. He retained as much of the moral regulations of the Jews and Christians as was best adapted to the life of nations in a warm climate. His political and military ability and his capacity for governing men were extraordinary. Savary was an enlightened Westerner, who, to be sure, justly refused to call Mohammed a prophet, but who was nevertheless forced to recognize him as one of the greatest men who ever lived.[1]

In 1742, in his tragedy, *Mahomet*, Voltaire advanced the exact opposite of this high evaluation of the personality of the Prophet. In his preface he attacks Boulainvilliers and Sale, declaring that had Mohammed been born a prince, or had he been called to power by the choice of the people, and had he established peaceful laws and defended his country against enemies, then it would be possible to honour him. But when a camel-dealer stirs up rebellion, claims to have conversed with Gabriel, and to have received this incomprehensible book, in which 'every page does violence to sober reason, when he murders men and abducts women in order to force them to believe in this book,' such conduct can be defended by no man 'unless he is born a Turk, or unless

[1] Savary, *Le Coran traduit de l'arabe précédé d'un abregé de la vie de Mahomet* ("Meque l'an de l'Hegire, 1163"), i, pp. 222-230.

superstition has choked all of the light of nature in him.' To be sure, Voltaire admits that Mohammed did not commit deliberately the villainies which his drama attributes to him, but a man 'who makes war against his own country, and who dares to do this in the name of God, is he not capable of anything?' In a later work, *Essai sur les mœurs*, Voltaire pronounced a somewhat milder judgment upon Mohammed, acknowledging his greatness and his abilities, but censuring his cruelty and brutality, and asserting that there is nothing new in his religion except the statement that Mohammed is the Apostle of Allah.

Voltaire's opinion became fashionable. Diderot claimed that Mohammed was the greatest friend of woman and the greatest enemy of sober reason who ever lived. On Friday, March 8, 1840, when Carlyle began his description of Mohammed's personality in his second lecture on "Heroes and Hero-Worship," he stated that the prevalent view was that Mohammed was an impostor, an incarnation of falsehood, and that his religion was a combination of charlatanism and stupidity. But in Carlyle's opinion such a view is a reflection upon ourselves. One hundred and eighty million human beings confess Islam as the true religion. For countless people Mohammed's words have been the guiding star of their lives. Can it be possible that so many creatures, created by God, have lived and died for something which must be regarded as a tragic fraud? What are we to think of this world, if charlatanism really has such power over the minds of men? This hypothesis is a sad creation of the age of scepticism, and is more indicative of mental paralysis and spiritual death. A more godless theory has never been propounded.

In Carlyle's opinion Mohammed was sincere, as every great man is sincere, because he had to be. He was genuinely sincere in spite of his deep consciousness of a lack of sincerity. The great fact of existence overwhelmed him; he could not escape its grip. Others might ignore this fact, and live in empty vanity, but to him the reality of life seemed terribly wonderful, and a flaming vision before his eyes. Such a man is a great man. We may also call him an original man, a messenger who brings us news of the infinite and the unknown. We might call him a poet or a prophet, for we feel that the words which he speaks are not the words of an ordinary man. They have their immediate source in the inner reality of things, since he lives in constant fellowship with this reality. For Carlyle's romantic idealism the man of genius is at once the highest revelation and the symbol of that Divine power which is the innermost reality of existence. Mohammed had seen the light of the Divine law of existence, 'a confused dazzling splendour of life and heaven, in the great darkness which threatened to be death: he called it revelation and the angel Gabriel—who of us yet can know what to call it?'

Mohammed's religious integrity rests, then, upon the fact that he himself was one of those great personalities who are expressions of the creative life of God, and who have, therefore, an intuitive contact with this creative life, a spontaneous revelation of God. The sacred book and the angel are only symbolical expressions of this experience of God, expressions which Carlyle evidently regards as rather unessential. In this respect the romantic philosophy of intuition adopts approximately the same point of view as that of the Enlightenment.

For us also the originality, the immediacy, and the freshness of religious experience may be proof of the genuineness of inspiration. Unfortunately, however, it depends very much upon the attitude of the observer, and his ability to enter sympathetically into the object, whether he will acknowledge the presence of this criterion. There are students of religion, even those who are not bound by doctrinal scruples, who cannot, in Carlyle's sense, discover anything genuine and immediate in Mohammed, even though they have the best of intentions. The problem of the subjective genuineness and integrity of religious inspiration is primarily a psychological problem. Unfortunately it is not impossible that the man who has received one or more genuine revelations may also produce consciously fraudulent messages, or appear on the scene as a religious charlatan with alleged miracles and feats of power. It may frequently be observed that the inspired man lives in an imaginary and unreal world, and that he has a decided tendency to recast trivial reality in terms of the mental dream-world in which his mind has its being. In such a case even the most penetrating psychological investigation is frequently unable to determine whether good faith and honesty, in the subjective sense, are present. It seems perfectly possible that an experience may be both genuine and spurious, and afterwards the inspired man may awaken, as from a dream, and will then be aware that he himself has produced the supernatural experiences.

On the other hand, it is unfair to assert that the tendency toward falsehood, deception, and pathological prevarication is a general characteristic of inspired men. The earlier medical psychology advanced this theory, and it has a natural basis in the fact that medical investigators were especially occupied with the pathological, inferior, and degenerate cases of inspiration. However, this alienation from reality, this form of introversion, may be combined with the highest degree of personal honesty. All of us have certainly met people of this type, incurable visionaries, dreamers who are in the world but who find it difficult to make contact with reality, and just as difficult to accept things as they are, and we have found that they are thoroughly honest people who quite courageously demand and proclaim the truth. On the other hand, people may be sober realists with a keen eye for detail, and yet be extremely cunning deceivers. It may even be doubted whether a fraud on the grand scale is possible without a keen sense of reality. This patent psychological fact has been overlooked by those who identify the tendency to falsification with an introverted escape from reality.

That Mohammed's inspiration was genuine in the psychological sense has already been emphasized incidentally. It is hardly believable that a man could have won such absolute confidence, or could have made such an impression upon his surroundings, had he not possessed an overwhelming and convincing faith in his own message. Mohammed regarded his call with the utmost sincerity; he felt his heart tremble before the King of the Judgment Day, and he responded to His prophetic commission with fear and trembling. 'But if Mohammed had fabricated concerning us any sayings, we had surely seized him by the right hand, and had cut through the vein of his neck. Nor would we have withheld any of you from him' (69, 44-47). Allah stations watchmen who walk before and behind His Apostle to make sure that he is faithfully transmitting His message. One need not be especially well disposed to the personal quality of a religious proclamation in order to hear the footsteps of these stern watchmen in the fearful warnings of the Prophet, as well as in the drastic expressions of his sorrow and perplexity when no one heeds his preaching.

Many inspired men have succeeded in performing signs and wonders which have confirmed their claim of a call. The legends of the miracles of holy men are not always fables created in a vacuum; they may often describe actual experiences, although these have undergone a peculiar reconstruction. Of course, such miracles are often produced in all subjective honesty, but we can readily understand how deception might be employed, either consciously or unconsciously. Mohammed rejected every request to pose as a wonder-worker, and emphatically denied all superstitions in regard to his own person. He is only a man like other men; he has no recourse to heavenly resources; he is not even the master of his own fate, to say nothing of the fate of others. To be sure, these statements originated in Mecca. But there is nothing to show that Mohammed attempted to exploit the superstitious reverence for his person which the believers in Medina are supposed to have shown him. At the most we might infer from Sura 66, 3 that he attempted to maintain the necessary discipline in his harem by letting it be known that he knew more than others. Perhaps this was a kind of pious fraud on his part, but it certainly occurred under mitigating circumstances. At all events, in important matters he did not attempt to advance his authority or safeguard his position by means of alleged miracles. I know of only two exceptions. The one occurred at Bedr, where he threw a handful of sand at the enemy in the belief that this magic act would help to gain the victory. And it seems quite understandable that in this moment of highest tension, when his cause really hung in the balance, he should receive a sign of such significance from Allah. In fact, it is just as natural as it was for Isaiah, who ordinarily never posed as a wonder-worker, to have no scruples about promising every sign which King Ahaz desired in order to win him over to his daring faith. The other exception is Mohammed's midnight journey to Jerusalem. This was a dream to which he seems to refer in such a way as to prove that he attributed to it the same validity that he attributed to other experiences.

Islamic dogma has depicted the Prophet as sinless. He never committed a deliberate sin, and at the most he may have been guilty only of some involuntary unintentional act which might be reckoned among the lighter sins. It is a likeable characteristic of Mohammed that he never claimed perfection or infallibility, but always admitted frankly that he was guilty of shortcomings and mistakes like other men. According to Sura 48, 1, the 'undoubted victory,' that is, the conquest of Mecca, is a sign that Allah has forgiven the Prophet his earlier and later sins. The touching story of the pearl necklace, which Mohammed gave to 'Ayesha, and which caused him a sleepless night, shows that, in spite of his lofty opinion of his position as the Apostle of Allah, he still retained something of that simplicity of heart characteristic of the upright man. Not once in his career did he feel invulnerable to errors and mistakes. That he was not disloyal to his holy task seems to him only an act of the special grace of God (17, 75-77). Like other prophets. Mohammed prayed: 'O our Lord! forgive us our sins and our mistakes in this our work; and set our feet firm; and help us against the unbelieving people' (3, 141). On the whole it may be said that Mohammed exhibited as much humility and self-criticism as one could reasonably expect from an Apostle of Allah whose work was crowned with such striking outward success. That he so resolutely withstood the temptations to pride and self-exaltation involved in his position shows that he was a man of moral sincerity.

In the problem of Mohammed's personal integrity is also involved the question of the extent to which he himself lived up to the religious and moral ideal which he created. He did not hesitate to set himself up as a model for believers; 'A noble pattern had ye in God's Apostle, for all who hope in God and in the latter days' (33, 21), just as St. Paul expressed the wish that his converts might become like him in all things except his chains. Such moral self-consciousness doubtless presupposes an absence of apparent contradiction between Mohammed's religious ideal of life and his personal conduct. His religious morality was on the whole of an ascetic nature. To be sure, the things of the world are not in themselves evil, but they easily become a snare and cause one to forget the world to come. Did Mohammed succeed in guarding himself from the temptations of the world, or did he fall a victim in Medina, as is frequently claimed, to temptations of power, honour, and enjoyment?

The oldest collections of tradition often depict the Prophet as an emaciated penitent. According to one writer, the habit of eating until one is satisfied was a new fad, unknown to the pious men of the first generation. The Prophet said: 'Adam's son filled no vessel which is more evil than his stomach'—and he acted accordingly. 'Ayesha relates that he never ate to satiety, and that he never asked for or desired food when he was with his wives. He ate and drank only what was given to him. The members of Mohammed's family lived in such poverty that they really suffered privation. Anas Ibn Malik, Mohammed's valet, tells that when Fatima once came to her father with bread, he said: 'This is the first bite which your father has tasted in three days.'[1] Abu Huraira, the authority for a great number of traditions which sound

[1] Nabhani, pp. 152 ff.

a strictly ascetic-pietistic note, relates that the Prophet became so hungry that he tightly bound his stomach and his loins in order to relieve his suffering.[1] The same writer states that month after month passed in Mohammed's family without a fire being kindled in the house to bake bread or pastry. 'Upon what do you live?' the questioner asked, and Abu Huraira answered: 'Upon the two black things: dates and water.'—'Ayesha tells how she once received a leg of lamb from her father, and how she and Allah's Apostle attempted to devour it in the dark—'In the dark?' asked the listeners; 'had you no lamps?'—'If we had had lamps we would have used up our oil long ago,' 'Ayesha replied.—On another occasion she suddenly burst into tears, and when those present asked why she wept, she answered: 'I have heard that you are now in the habit of eating yourself so full that you need medicine in order to heal your stomachs. Then I thought of your Prophet. As long as he lived he never filled his stomach with two kinds of food. When he ate his fill of dates, then he ate no bread. When he satisfied his hunger with bread, then he ate no dates.[2] When the Prophet died he had put his coat of mail in pawn with a Jew for three measures of meal.[3] Another tradition tells of his simplicity and his freedom from pretension. 'When Allah sent Mohammed He said: "This is My Prophet, My elect, accept him as a friend and obey his rules and ways. No portals prevent access to him and no guard stands in the way. No large keys are brought to him in the morning and at night. He clothes himself in rough garments, rides upon a donkey, and licks his fingers after he has eaten." He says: "Whoever is not willing to follow my *Sunna* does not belong to me." '[4]

Some of these stories seem to be fairly true to life, and evidently bear the marks of realistic description. But we become sceptical when we find other traditions which present

1 Ibn Sa'd, i, 2, p. 114.
2 Ibn Sa'd, i, 2, pp. 117-118.
3 Bukhari and Muslim, compare Nabhani, p. 153.
4 Ibn Sa'd, i, 2, p. 95.

an entirely different picture of the Prophet, and emphatically deny that he practised an ascetic ideal. It is told that some of the companions of the Prophet boasted of their pious works in his presence. One man said: 'I am unmarried,' another: 'I eat no meat,' a third: 'I sleep on the bare ground,' and a fourth: 'I fast continually.' Then Mohammed said: 'Praise be to Allah! I fast and I eat, I keep vigil and I sleep, and I am married. And whoever is not willing to follow my *Sunna* does not belong to me.'[1] The attempt is made to show that the Prophet lived like an ordinary man. There was nothing of bigotry or of the hyper-spiritual in his nature. Several pious men came to Zaid Ibn Thabit and said: 'Tell us about the characteristics of the Prophet.' He answered: 'I was his neighbour, and when the revelation came to him I wrote it down for him. When we conversed about this world he also spoke of it, and when we conversed about food, he also spoke of that. Do you desire that I should tell you all about that?'[2]

In these contrasting statements we actually have, then, not so much descriptions of the circumstances of the domestic life of Mohammed as formal principles relating to ethical questions, along with the attempt to illuminate and support these principles by appealing to the authority of the Prophet's exemplary life. In Islam there were pious men of strict habits, pietists and ascetics, who wished to follow the narrow road of abstinence, and they fought against every form of worldly-mindedness and fleshly desire. Others were of the opinion that one ought to be temperate in one's piety and participate in some of the joys of life. Hence what the traditions tell us about Mohammed's private life is comparatively worthless as a historical source.

This much is certain, however, that the descriptions of the poverty and deprivations of the Prophet must be greatly exaggerated. According to Wakidi, the fifth part of all the spoils of war which the Prophet received as his share was used partly for gifts and alms, but also for the support of

[1] Ibn Sa'd, i, 2, p. 113.
[2] *Ibid.*, p. 90.

his family, so that if he could present 'Ayesha with a costly pearl necklace he would not need to pawn his coat of mail. He probably did not live such a completely simple life as the pious romanticism of the legend supposes. Judging by various passages of the Koran, in Medina Mohammed tried to invest himself with a kind of ceremonial to emphasize his new rôle as ruler. For example, he forbids the believers 'to raise their voices before the Prophet,' that is, to speak loudly in his presence, and he warns them not to indulge in familiar conversation in his presence. He was not content simply to command what good form demanded, namely, that no one should enter his house without first asking permission, but in order to decrease the crowd of complaining petitioners he probably prescribed a certain fee, in the form of voluntary alms for the general treasury, for those seeking admission to his presence. This regulation, and the repeal of it which immediately followed, is one of the queerest passages in the Koran. The regulation is found in Sura 58, 13: 'O ye who believe! when ye go to confer in private with the Apostle, give alms before such conference. Better will this be for you and purer. But if ye have not the means, then truly God is lenient, merciful.' Then there follows immediately: 'Do ye hesitate to give alms previously to your private conference? Then if ye do it not (and God will excuse it in you), at least observe prayer, and pay the stated impost, and obey God and His Apostle.' This seems to us to be a quite disgraceful capitulation. A man who can risk such a wild leap without injuring his prestige must obviously be in very good standing with his believers. The Arabic commentaries relate that this regulation remained in force only for one hour, or—what seems more probable—only for ten days. The poor had nothing to give, the wealthy did not want to give anything, so they all ceased trying to obtain conferences with the Prophet. Ali boasted of being the only one who obeyed the rule: he gave a dirhem (a silver coin worth about 17 cents) for every conversation.[1] In another tradition Ali appears in a less favourable light.[2] The Prophet asked him what he thought of the fee; whether a dinar (a gold coin worth about 5 dollars) would be fair. Ali answered: 'The believers cannot pay so much.' Mohammed countered: 'Then what do you suggest?' Ali replied: 'A kernel of wheat or a grain of barley would be sufficient.' 'You are truly moderate,' said the Prophet. No doubt such little attempts to establish a type of court ceremonial did not appeal to the freedom-loving and unaffected Bedouin. The motive prompting the Prophet was primarily a desire to demand respect and discipline, this being more than necessary at this time, when new groups of believers were being added, in whom the religious reverence for the personality of the Prophet was none too deeply rooted.

There is every indication, however, that even in Medina Mohammed lived on the whole in rather modest circumstances, and adhered to the moderately ascetic ideal which he defends in the Koran. We are there told that he defended himself against all possible accusations of the Jews or 'hypocrites,' and of the doubters among the population of Medina. But there is no mention of complaints concerning luxury, splendour, or high living. Therefore we are right in assuming that the life of the Prophet presented no occasion for criticism on this point. And we should not forget that the stricter groups, who, especially during the rule of the Umayyads, championed the older ascetic-pietistic order in opposition to a growing worldliness, were apparently the rightful heirs of the inner circle of the companions of the Prophet, who, in contrast to the young, proud fortune-seekers of the Meccan nobility, treasured and observed not only his political but also his religious ideals—men like Umar, Abu Huraira, Ibn Mas'ud, and others. The piety which characterizes the sincere

[1] Hibatallah Ibn Salama, *Kitab al-nasikh wal-mansukh* (in the margin of Wakidi, *Asbab al-nazul*, Cairo, 1916), pp. 298 ff.

[2] Tabari, Tafsir to sura 58, 13.

believers of the first generation is certainly derived from the basic religious attitude of the Prophet himself.

The genuineness and sincerity of Mohammed's piety, and the honesty of his belief in his religious call, are indisputable. Unfortunately it cannot be said that righteousness and straightforwardness are the most prominent traits of his character as a whole. We have already cited examples, like the Nakhla expedition and the murder of Ka'b Ibn Al-Ashraf, and there are similar cases which sometimes show a very repulsive leaning toward craftiness and trickery. However, an analysis of Mohammed's character proves that certain things can and should be said in his defence. At first he seems to be dominated by a native slyness which is not uncommon in an introvert type of temperament. Such a person often possesses a richly developed emotional and imaginative life, but suffers from a certain fear of action, or rather, from a fear of direct contact with brutal reality. This slyness is not identical with weakness of character and will, and it has nothing to do with a pathological paralysis of the will. On the contrary, people of this type may have exceptionally strong will-power, the ability to carry out a plan with stern indomitable consistency, and an amount of energy by which the noisy and reckless daredevil temperaments are ultimately put to shame. The late president of the Theosophical Society, Annie Besant, was a good recent example of this. She was undoubtedly a born ruler, and the possessor of phenomenal endurance, industry, and energy. She tells us that at first she suffered from unusual shyness and reserve in her contacts with people. Not until she mounted the platform to speak was she gripped by an enthusiasm which gave her invincible and reckless courage. Mohammed, who, when he recited his revelations publicly, attacked the idolatry and worldliness of his countrymen without the least hesitation, really seems to have been the victim of a certain inner uncertainty in personal relations, and of an inability to speak openly and frankly express his opinion. Like St. Paul, he is strong and mighty in words but 'his bodily presence is weak.' When the spoils are being divided we see the unbridled Bedouin pressing in upon Allah's Apostle, yelling and even tearing at his clothes, until finally the stern Umar, with his riding-whip and his commanding, fear-inspiring voice, demanded respect for Allah's Apostle. In the presence of the Prophet a man once assailed Abu Bekr in terms of violent scorn. Mohammed remained silent, and when Abu Bekr began to defend himself the Prophet went away. When Abu Bekr afterwards reproached him for his behaviour, he declared that Gabriel had been refuting the assailant all along, but that the angel departed when Abu Bekr began to defend himself. Another no less delightful story tells that 'Ayesha reproached the Prophet because he first spoke in very disparaging terms of a certain person, but that when this man came in later on Mohammed greeted him with exceptional courtesy. A man who lacks the ability to speak frankly like a robust and straightforward person is easily tempted to accomplish his will by the use of cunning and trickery.

According to the tradition of Islam, the Prophet's personality was characterized by unique kindliness, amiability, and friendliness. He was never the first to withdraw his hand when he greeted anyone, and he was never the first to turn his face away when conversing with another. No one, whether a red man or a black (that is, an Arab or a negro) ever spoke to him without receiving a reply, and he often picked up discarded dates and put them into his mouth because he thought that they might be a gift and did not wish to offend the giver. He greeted everyone, slaves and little children as well. When 'Ayesha was questioned as to the conduct of the Prophet in private life, she replied: 'The most gentle and noble of men. Otherwise he was like other men, except that he loved to laugh and smile.'[1] It is surely no accident that our sources so often refer to this irresistible smile. It is evident that Mohammed had a remarkable gift for winning people. Often, as with a magic stroke, he succeeded in transforming dissatisfaction into surrender and dislike into attraction. He showed special kindness to his former enemies; such

[1] Ibn Sa'd, i, 2, p. 91.

friendliness, in fact, that it sometimes arouses the anger of his friends. It seems to have been most natural for Mohammed to try to win men through friendliness and accommodation, and few were able to resist his personal charm. His tendency to yield as far as possible in respect of the regulations and laws which he himself had instituted bear witness to the same characteristics. His forbearance is not due to a weak complaisance, but to the fact that by nature it was hard for him to look upon complaining and dissatisfied faces. A distinct desire to remain popular, celebrated, and beloved, is a weakness which seems to be associated with the gift of inspiration. The seers have this in common with artists and poets. To be sure, an analysis of this desire may reveal other than moral motives. An unfriendly observer will detect in it an exaggerated passion for self-assertion, human vanity, softness, and over-sensitivity. It cannot be denied that this type of personality indicates a certain tendency to neglect old friendships and loyalties in order to seek perpetually for new conquests, a lack of consideration and a coldness toward the best of friends, and a rather weak amiability toward enemies. The good qualities which stand out are a strong social instinct, a love of personal fellowship, unsolicited friendliness, and accessibility. It may be said, therefore, in Mohammed's defence, that the art of dissimulation already mentioned is based in part upon a natural urge to conceal anger and dissatisfaction behind a mask of friendliness.

Finally, we should not forget that the political game definitely requires a certain perfection in the art of dissimulation. *Qui scit dissimulare, scit regnare*—'the man who can conceal his ideas knows how to rule'—is a formula which Aeneas Sylvius (Pius II) ascribes to the Emperor Sigismund. Moreover, the great self-control which Mohammed could practise when he desired was a natural pre-requisite to his becoming an outstanding politician.

No doubt the trait of Mohammed's character most offensive to the Christian Occident is his sensuality. His lack of moderation and control in this sphere appears worse to us because the common-sense Christian morality, being an heir of the ancient asceticism, is based on an exaggerated idea of the sinfulness of the sexual instinct. Offences in this sphere are often regarded as *the* sin in an absolute and real sense. But even the Jews in Medina found Mohammed's conduct to be offensive in this respect, and they asked: 'What kind of Prophet is this man who only thinks of marrying?' Undoubtedly a prophet who declares that women and children belong to the enticements of worldly life, and who nevertheless accumulates a harem of nine wives, in addition to various slave-women, is a strange phenomenon when regarded from the standpoint of morality. The situation is not improved by the fact that up to Khadijah's death, that is, until Mohammed was fifty years old, he was content with one wife. At the height of his career, when he was already an ageing man, he gave free rein to his sensual impulses.

Nevertheless, we cannot judge the Prophet of Islam according to our moral standards, but only according to the standards which he himself recognized. And in order to understand his attitude in this matter we must before all things know the background, the moral conditions in Arabia at the time of his appearance, the basis upon which his sexual ethics developed. In Mohammed's day endogamy was generally practised among the Arabs—that is, a wife was taken from one's own tribe. To be sure, there are also traces of exogamy, and this fact has been taken, perhaps incorrectly, as proof of an original matriarchy. This explains why it could happen that a man married into the family of the woman, and remained there as a guest (*jar*), where he was under the protection of, and usually economically dependent upon, her family. It might also happen that he remained in his own tribe and only occasionally visited his wife. In this case he might also make similar alliances in other tribes. In these exogamous marriages the woman was the determining factor, and could initiate a divorce. If she wanted to get rid of her husband she turned the flap of the tent toward another side when she anticipated his visit. He took the hint, and reconciled himself to the inevitable without further ado. However, it was more customary for a man to marry a woman of his own tribe when he did not obtain a wife as part of the spoils of war. In such an endogamous marriage the man was absolutely the superior, and could promptly divorce his wife or take her back if he chose. She was his property, and the only restriction upon his right of disposal was that he could not sell her. On the other hand, if she had been disloyal to him he could kill her without being punished.

It is no wonder that sexual morality was on a low level, judged by our standards. Polygamy was customary, the number of wives might be as large as a man pleased, and divorces were effected without any ceremony. The children were regarded as belonging to the man to whom they were born and to the tribe. The ancient Arabs do not seem to have been burdened with moral sensitivity in sexual matters. It might happen that a man would lend his wife to an especially brave and prominent man in order to beget children of good stock. Less permanent alliances also were regarded as completely legitimate within certain limits. This is true of the so-called *mut'a* alliance, or temporary marriage. This form of legalized vice, which meets the demand for a simpler and more convenient form of marriage, is advocated also by certain reformers of our own day. It provides that a couple may enter into a relationship for a specified period of time, at least for one day. The man makes a gift, which in this case belongs to the woman and not to her guardian, but otherwise such a temporary marriage involves no legal consequences. According to some authorities Sura 4, 28, which was given during the expedition of conquest to Mecca, is supposed to contain an approval of temporary marriage. If Mohammed really made such a concession for a time, then it was a chance surrender to a pagan custom, which at that time was regarded as completely permissible and correct. According to Damiri, a man named Sirin relates the following story: 'When the permission was granted for the *mut'a* marriage, I and a comrade went to a girl of the Bedouin tribe Banu 'Amr who looked like a long-necked female camel. When we courted her she asked: "What shall I receive as a bridal gift?" Each one of us offered his cloak. My comrade's cloak was finer, but I was younger than he. The girl examined the cloak of my comrade and admitted that it was beautiful. Then she looked at me and took me and my poor cloak. We were married for three days until Allah's Apostle withdrew his permission."[1]

When Mohammed's sensuality is seen against the background of such a conception of the ethics of marriage it appears in a different light. It is a very uncertain whether his Arabian contemporaries found his conduct in this matter to be in any way notorious or unfitting. With apparent amusement the earliest tradition recalls 'Ayesha's clever sayings about her husband's weakness for the opposite sex, and it candidly repeats the saying of the Prophet that women, pleasant odours, and prayer are the three things which he has found most precious in this world. It may perhaps be thought that a criticism on the part of the believers led to the restriction of erotic freedom which Mohammed imposes upon himself in Sura 33, 52. For here it is stated that from now on it is not permitted to the Prophet to take women as wives, even though their beauty please him. It is possible that a certain dissatisfaction with his personal privileges in this matter prevailed. But it is more likely that this restriction was a concession to the wives of the Prophet with whom he had just had an altercation, for some reason of which we have no certain knowledge, and on which occasion he had declared his intention of divorcing them all.

In defence of Mohammed, it should be said that he faithfully observed his own restrictions, and that he sought to control intemperate licence in sexual matters by legislation. He tried in various ways to inculcate a more ethical conception of marriage, and to raise the position of women, for example, by a legal determination of the right of inheritance, which previously had been only casually recognized,

[1] Kitab al-hayawan, i, p. 21.

and by the requirement that women should be treated with kindness, friendliness, and justice.

In spite of everything that can be said in defence of Mohammed's religious integrity and his loyalty to his call, his endurance, his liberality, and his generosity, we are not doing the Prophet of Islam an injustice when we conclude that this moral personality does not stand upon the same level with his other endowments; and indeed, not even upon the same level with his religious endowments. But if we would be fair to him we must not forget that, consciously or unconsciously, we Christians are inclined to compare Mohammed with the unsurpassed and exalted figure whom we meet in the Gospels, and that we cannot avoid seeing his historical personality against the background of the perfect moral ideal to which the faith of his followers tried to exalt him. And when it is measured by such a standard, what personality is not found wanting?

INDEX

INDEX

INDEX